WOMEN WHO DATE TOO MUCH

(And Those Who Should Be So Lucky)

 A Guide For Singles in Search of Significant Others

LINDA SUNSHINE

Illustrations by Richard Stine

NAL BOOKS

NEW AMERICAN LIBRARY

NEW YORK AND SCARBOROUGH, ONTARIO

Published simultaneously in Canada by The New American Library of
Canada Limited.

The author gratefully acknowledges the following permissions:

Passages reprinted by permission of Avon Books from SEX AND THE SINGLE
GIRL by Helen Gurley Brown. Copyright © 1962 by Helen Gurley Brown.

Speech from THE BIG CHILL by Lawrence Kasdan and Barbara Benedek.
Copyright © 1987 by Columbia Pictures Industries, Inc. St. Martin's Screenplay
Series, St. Martin's Press, Inc., New York.

 NAL BOOKS TRADEMARK REG. U.S. PAT. OFF. AND FOREIGN COUNTRIES
REGISTERED TRADEMARK—MARCA REGISTRADA
HECHO EN CHICAGO, U.S.A.

SIGNET, SIGNET CLASSIC, MENTOR, ONYX, PLUME, MERIDIAN
and NAL BOOKS are published in the United States by NAL PENGUIN INC.,
1633 Broadway, New York, New York 10019,
and in Canada by The New American Library of Canada Limited,
81 Mack Avenue, Scarborough, Ontario M1L 1M8

Library of Congress Cataloging-in-Publication Data

Sunshine, Linda.
    Women who date too much (and those who should be so
lucky).

    1. Dating (Social customs)—Anecdotes, facetiae,
satire, etc.   2. Single women—United States—
Psychology—Anecdotes, facetiae, satire, etc.
3. Mate selection—United States—Anecdotes, facetiae,
satire, etc.   4. Interpersonal relations—Anecdotes,
facetiae, satire, etc.   I. Title.
HQ801.S94   1988   646.7'7   87-24841
ISBN 0-453-00608-6

Designed by Leonard Telesca

First Printing, May, 1988

1   2   3   4   5   6   7   8   9

PRINTED IN THE UNITED STATES OF AMERICA

Dedicated to my dear friend Jean Holabird
for arranging my last two blind dates.
Thanks, I think.

Acknowledgments
Special thanks to Richard Stine, Meredith Bernstein, Gary Luke, Arnold Dolin, Adam Scott Dorenter, and his friends at County Road School, for putting my picture on their classroom bulletin board, right next to the two–headed turtle.

A Note on the Illustrations
In my opinion, Richard Stine is one of the greatest illustrators on the planet Earth. Fortunately for all of us, his illustrations are available on note cards and some are sold as prints. If you can't find them in your local card store, or if you want more information on Stine's prints, cards, and books, contact: Palomar Press, P.O. Box 1124, Ojai, CA 93023.

Contents

Preface

How I Came to Write This Book

 Some of us are becoming the men we wanted to marry.

—*Gloria Steinem*

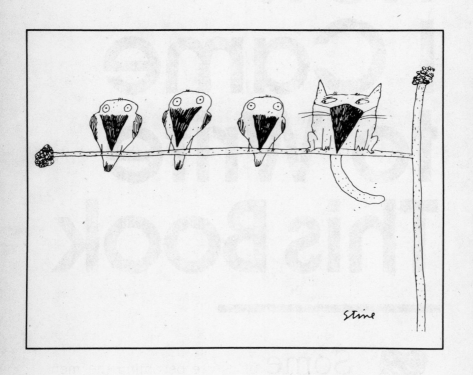

Stine

It was the afternoon of December 31. I was sitting at home waiting for my new boyfriend to call. His name wasn't Jim, but that's what I'll call him.[1]

Jim was as close to perfection as I'd found, although, truthfully, I had to admit, I didn't know him very well. Yet Jim had passed the "S" test: he was single, straight, successful, and sexy, which was as close to a miracle as one could expect these days.

Jim and I had met three weeks ago. We'd had four dates. I was trying hard not to rush things, although I had already selected a name for our firstborn.

I was relatively certain Jim would ask me out for New Year's Eve even though he only had about eight hours left until midnight struck. I kept reminding myself to give Jim the benefit of the doubt, and that eight hours was almost enough time for me to get dressed.

The phone rang and I raced to answer it. It was my agent, Meredith.

I tried not to sound disappointed as I listened to Meredith explain she'd just come from lunch with a publisher who

---

[1] His name was Joel Aaron Fargoet, 745 East 83rd Street, New York, New York 10014. Age: 42. Height: 6 feet. Weight: 173. Social Security Number: 151-39-9695. Shirt size: 15½-34.

wanted a writer for a humorous book about dating. Would I consider the project?

I told her I was expecting an important call and couldn't talk, but I'd think about it.

"Great," she said. "I've set up a meeting the day after tomorrow to discuss the idea."

I agreed to meet with her and the publisher and hung up the phone. Thinking about dating, I realized I was something of an expert on the subject, considering I had almost twenty years of on-the-job training. The thought made me depressed, which, of course, made me hungry. I switched on the answering machine and ran to the deli across the street. (Even important phone calls can wait for takeout.)

I stood at the counter, ordered my usual (tuna surprise on rye to go), and eavesdropped on the conversation between two young women at a booth near the counter.

"New Year's Eve just ain't a holiday for singles," sighed the woman with a head of hair that looked like it was styled with a Cuisinart (speed setting: Pulverized). "Of course, it ain't so great if you're married either. I mean you stare across the table at this *person* and you wonder—how'd I get stuck with *him* for another year?

"No, New Year's is only good if you've just met someone and you're falling in love."

I think about Jim and feel smug. Sandwich in hand, I rush back to my apartment. The phone is ringing.

It's him!

We chitchat for a few minutes before Jim gets down to business. He's calling to tell me he's getting involved with another woman and, as a one-woman guy, he feels guilty about us. He says he doesn't think we should see each other anymore.

I ask, "Does this mean you're not asking me out for New Year's?"

"I guess not. I already have a date tonight," he informs me.
"With who?"

"With this woman, the one I've been telling you about.
She's a doctor. We met three months ago through a singles ad
in *New York* magazine."

"Well, fine, Jim," I say. "I could tell you I hope it'll work
out but I'd be lying. So, good-bye and have a nice life."

"Gee, you make it sound so final," he says.

"It is."

"We'll run into each other again."

"Not if I can help it," I say.

I hang up the phone and have a long cry. I take a bath. I try
to write poetry. I make myself a cup of tea. I eat everything in
the kitchen, including a small jar of mayonnaise.

When I wake up two days later my eyes are still puffy, my
nose is stuffed, and my stomach bloated. I don't think I could
feel any worse. Then I realize I have to get dressed and go to
a meeting where I'm expected not only to be bright and
chipper but to make jokes about being single. This is the story
of my life, I think, as I pull the covers over my head.

Eventually, I get out of bed and walk into the kitchen to
make a cup of coffee, where I notice Jim's business card
tacked on my bulletin board. I rip it to shreds.

What's funny about dating? I ask the world outside my
window.

Two hours later, I'm in the publisher's office with my
agent. Luckily, she's being bright and chipper and making
jokes.

I'm thinking about Jim, rewording in my mind our conversation so that I sound like the one who's dumping him. It's a
stretch, even with my aptitude for fantasy.

The publisher smiles at me. "So, are you interested in our
idea?" he asks.

"Can I write a chapter on revenge?"

"Why not?" says the publisher.

"On holding a grudge?"

"Uh, I guess so."

"On being celibate?"

My agent kicks me under the table.

The publisher scratches his head. "We are talking about a *humor* book, right?"

My agent laughs. "She's just kidding. Really."

I wasn't, but never mind.

My friend Lee, the astrologer, says, "There's a gift in everything." And, I guess the gift here is that I get to write a book and make a profit off Jim and all the other guys who've inadvertently provided me with material for this book.

Fine, but just don't ask me if I'd trade the book, the contract, and my agent for a date with Jim.

Excuse me, but I've got to go get something to eat.

L. Sunshine
Burger King, New York City
5/17/87

The History of Dating

 Time is nature's way of keeping everything from happening all at once.

—*Unknown*

 No one should have to dance backwards all their lives.

—*Jill Ruckelshaus, New York Times,
August 3, 1973*

The Perpetual Enigma

The Wedding March of Civilization: Dating from Adam and Eve to Madonna and Sean

Mankind's first official attempt at dating took place in the Garden of Eden, and, like most dates, it was based on a profound misunderstanding.

Adam was eating breakfast one morning when he spied a young woman staring at him from behind a rubber tree. Upon

stine

closer inspection, Adam thought he detected a certain hungry look in this strange creature's eyes, so he kindly offered her a piece of his fruit. "Wanna date?" Adam asked.

Eve, the original single woman, heard opportunity knocking loud and clear. "You bet," she said. "Let's do lunch." And she rushed off to wash her hair.

Historians note that the phenomenon of dating might've been radically altered if Adam had been eating a grapefruit that fateful morning.

But he wasn't, and, as we know, Adam and Eve continued to "date"—on and off—for the remainder of their lives, which wasn't all that difficult considering Eve had virtually no competition in Eden and millions of years would pass before the discovery of cellulite.

Throughout the Ages we now call Stone, Ice, Bronze, and Iron, dating consisted mainly of informal gatherings for the purpose of hunting and foraging (sort of like Woodstock in a fur coat). Romance during this time was minimal, since primitive man had yet to create Snoopy greeting cards. In fact, nothing much happened until the scientific discovery of astrology, which altered the course of dating by enabling single men to introduce themselves by asking: "What's your sign?"

The next momentous event in dating history is credited to Cleopatra, the Queen of Egypt. After her boyfriend, Caesar, was assassinated, Cleo began fooling around with Marcus Antonius, her best friend's husband. Thus, Cleopatra became the first woman in recorded history to date a married man. Like many such relationships, this one ended badly. Cleopatra committed suicide at age thirty-nine.

Centuries passed and dating took a back seat to lots and lots of wars—at least until the French Revolution, when things picked up, thanks to Marie Antoinette. A genuine boy toy, Marie liked to mix heavy necking and whipped cream, a combination that greatly aroused Louis XVI and, more importantly, was the method by which the couple inadvertently invented French kissing. Unbeknownst to Louis, Marie demonstrated their discovery to almost every garçon at Versailles, which is probably why dating enjoyed a healthy revival in the late 1700s.

During the 1800s, several technological advances radically altered the course of dating. In 1824, the process of binding rubber to cloth was first patented. This seemingly innocuous event would subsequently lead to the invention of the girdle, a garment that almost single-handedly wiped dating off the face of the earth.

In 1865, George Pullman built his first railway sleeping car, thereby creating a reason to take a date along on a business trip. It wasn't long before people began making out in other moving vehicles as well. In fact, Pullman's early efforts probably account for the popularity of airplane bathrooms among today's traveling singles (hence the advertising slogan, "Fly United!").

In 1871, the typewriter was invented, which didn't directly affect dating per se but did permit me to write this sentence without using quill and ink.

In 1907, the Model T Ford was mass-produced for the first time, enabling everyone to own a car. This was important, because how else could people get to the drive-in?

No one would dispute that the most momentous—and timesaving—contribution to dating took place in 1915 with the invention of the zipper.

What is disputed, however, is the exact moment in history when the word "relationship" crept into our dating vocabulary. Attempting to discover the origin of this term, researchers have studied hundreds of tapes of the *Dating Game*, but all to no avail.

Scholars have noted, coincidentally, that their inability to determine when a "date" became a "relationship" is the same dilemma that confuses most single men today.

Yet no discussion of dating would be complete without evaluating, in some detail, the seminal singles book of our century, *Sex and the Single Girl*, which was published in May 1963 and, almost instantly, became one of the most talked about books of its time. Reviewed extensively, the intrinsic intellectual value of this book was perhaps best described by Miss Joan Crawford who stated: "It [this book] should be on every man's bed table—when he's free, that is." (For further information about how Helen Gurley Brown boosted the social life of the unavailable man, see chapter on "Dating Married Men.")

As proof of its relevance to modern-day society, *Sex and the Single Girl* was made into a movie starring Tony Curtis and Natalie Wood.

In the following paragraph from her book, Mrs. Brown displays a remarkable talent for deep psychological insight into the inner workings of the male psyche.

"When a man thinks of a single woman," writes Mrs. Brown, "he pictures her alone in her apartment, smooth legs sheathed in pink silk Capri pants, lying tantalizingly among dozens of satin cushions, trying to read but not very successfully, for *he* is in that room—filling her thoughts, her dreams, her life."

While parts of *Sex and the Single Girl* have become somewhat dated (Who can afford to live alone anymore? Who has smooth legs?), a great deal of the book, particularly Mrs. Brown's sound advice, has remained, surprisingly, as refreshingly and frankly applicable to today's single gal as it was for the swinging sixties gal of long ago. Take, for instance, the following examples of Helen Gurley Brown's wisdom:

- There are three kinds of people you absolutely must have in your single life: a really good butcher, a crack car mechanic, and a rich and powerful married couple.

- Demand and inspire expensive gifts from your dates. These are the rewards of single life.

- If he asks to go Dutch treat on your date, don't stand on ceremony. Dump him immediately.

As for me, my favorite piece of advice from *Sex and the Single Girl* involves not sex, but office politics. Over and over, Mrs. Brown stresses the importance of having a solid career and competing in the marketplace on an equal footing with men. In this way, perhaps Mrs. Brown could be considered a forerunner of *Ms.* magazine. Take, for example, the following piece of advice, which most certainly helped Gloria Steinem (and others like her) catapult up the corporate ladder. "About every six weeks several girls from my office and I round up all our clothes that need altering, and we gossip and sew for the evening. Isn't that jolly?"

While this idea strikes me as a wonderful way to finally get those loose buttons fixed on my raincoat, the other female executives in my office were not very receptive to the suggestion. So far, no one seems interested in a jolly evening of sewing and girl talk.

The decline in the popularity of sewing circles among female co-workers is, perhaps, not the only difference in the social life of a single woman in the days of *Sex and the Single Girl* and today. If someone were writing a late 1980s version of Helen Gurley Brown's opus (and I'm applying for the job), she might have to title the book *Sex and the Significant Other*. (Actually, in writing about my social life, the more appropriate title might be *Sex and the Insignificant Other*, but that's another story altogether.)

In other scholarly endeavors, researchers have studied the two most popular sex books of the past few decades in order to examine the sexual preferences of modern times. In the early 1970s, millions of copies of *Everything You Always Wanted to Know About Sex But Were Afraid to Ask* were sold; in the late 1970s, the best-selling book was entitled *The Joy of Sex*. We can deduce from these facts that, as we moved into the latter part of the last decade, people preferred books with shorter titles.

In the 1980s, many scholars maintain that the quintessential description of today's dating patterns can be found in the seminal singles movie, *The Big Chill*; more specifically, in Meg's speech after we learn that William Hurt isn't going to father her child. (A fact that would depress the hell out of any single gal.)

"They're either married or gay," Meg observes about the men in her life. "And if they're not gay, they've just broken up with the most wonderful woman in the world or they've just broken up with a bitch who looks exactly like me. They're in transition from a monogamous relationship and they need more space or they're tired of space but they just can't commit or they want to commit but they're afraid to get close. They want to get close and you don't want to get near them."

Scholars point out that this speech has been validated by a recent Harvard survey, which concluded that women in their late thirties and early forties have about as much chance of getting married as they do of winning the New York State Lottery twice in a row.

Part of this problem stems from the fact that there are lots

more single women than single men in today's dating pool
(which may account for why so many single gals are drowning
in despair of ever meeting Mr. Right). The chart on page 16
details the ratio of single men to single women in New York
City. (Manhattan is considered a mecca for singles, being one
of the few cities in the country where even the mayor is single
and apparently, on most Saturday nights, dateless.)

These figures were compiled by the Singles Census Bureau, which is a group also known as Anxious Mothers of
Single Daughters in Manhattan (AMOSDIM), which tracks
the number of single men and holds a formal wake every time
one of them marries.

Experts report that the reasons for the increasing number
of single women in the late 1980s are psychological, social,
and demographic and include the following:

- Many women are working at good jobs and supporting
  themselves. However, because women's salaries are still
  well below men's, economics does play an important
  factor in women's decisions to remain single. Because of
  their comparatively limited incomes, women are hesitant
  to get married and take on the additional financial bur-
  den of supporting a husband and, perhaps, children.

- Men classified as unmarried by the Census Bureau are
  often not interested in getting married, even when women
  spend a fortune on leg-waxing and Joy. In fact, many of
  these men prefer to reserve the leg-waxing appointments
  and the perfume for themselves.

- Many single women in their thirties and forties are only
  attracted to unavailable men, spending a good deal of
  their potentially marriageable years in love with their
  married bosses or their psychiatrists. Thus, these women

People Living Alone in New York City—1987

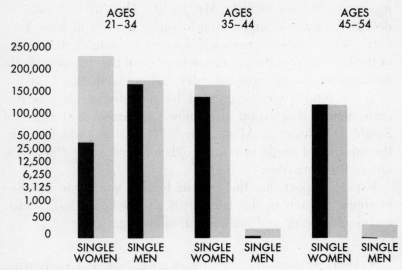

= Population of single women and single men in New York City.

= Part of population of single women and single men in New York City wanting to marry.

| AGE GROUP | TOTAL OF: | | TOTAL OF: | |
| | SINGLE WOMEN | SINGLE MEN | SINGLE WOMEN | SINGLE MEN |
			THAT WANT TO MARRY	
21–34	235,986	186,658	27,986	156,987
35–44	167,890	156	127,890	2*
45–54	134,879	234	134,879	.05**

*NOTE: These two men are Sam Debittle from Queens and Marty Cain from Brooklyn.

**NOTE: Gus Trambone, a 53-year-old bachelor from Valley Stream, claims he might be available if he could only find a "gal who's really loaded and who cooks as good as my mommy."

have greatly decreased their chances of ever finding a companion to join them in the matrimonial state.

- Women born in the baby-boom years had the misfortune of entering their early to mid-twenties at a very critical moment in American history. Specifically, these women came of marriageable age during the first broadcasts of *The Mary Tyler Moore Show*. The enormous popularity of the show encouraged these women to stay home on Saturday night and watch television instead of going out on blind dates, thus greatly decreasing their chances of snagging a husband. In addition, these women were brainwashed by the blatant propaganda promoted by the show, namely that it was okay to be single, as long as you were real skinny and had funny neighbors. It wasn't until these baby boomers hit their late thirties and early forties that it dawned on them that Mary Tyler Moore, in real life, was married to a successful Jewish doctor sixteen years her junior. Many women have never fully recovered from this crushing revelation.

Today's single women are a breed apart from the single women of Helen Gurley Brown's generation. No longer labeled a Jolly Spinster, the modern single gal is likely to own her own co-op or condo and to have learned not to feel out of place with her married friends and relatives. These women usually have a good relationship with children, either of their friends or siblings. Often they have challenging jobs and many social advantages. Their lives are wholly successful even though the vast majority of them are unbelievably depressed most of the time.

In order to get a first-hand account of the dating scene and how it affects the modern woman, this reporter recently attended a gathering of single women who congregated at the

Dew Drop Inn in Massapequa, New York, to discuss their social lives with the media. The room was filled to capacity with unmarried women, all of whom wore T-shirts that read: "I'd rather be married, or at least dating someone special." In the crowded room, this reporter noted that the ticking of biological clocks was almost deafening.

When asked about the problems of their social life, most of the women sounded confused and bitter.

"What can I say? It's the pits," claimed Tiffany Detroit, a thirty-four-year-old kindergarten teacher from Brooklyn. "I never meet any guys over five years old."

"At least they're single," countered a twenty-nine-year-old hairdresser who asked to remain anonymous. "You sound like you're in a great location to meet unmarried guys. The only men I meet on the job are the ones with better makeup than me."

Women at this meeting acknowledged that the holidays and the weekends were the hardest times for them. Several women reported working on Sunday in order to avoid seeing all the couples and married families having brunch or walking on the street.

"I like to spend time pampering myself on the weekends," claimed another single woman who also asked that her name be withheld. "I get into a hot bathtub on Friday night and I don't get out again until I have to go to work on Monday morning."

"Aren't you as wrinkled as an old prune by then, Betty Martin?" this reporter inquired.

"You bitch!" Betty screamed. "I told you not to mention my name!"

With a few exceptions, most of the women at the bar expressed regret that they would probably not have children of their own. "I'll never be able to manipulate a child the way Mom manipulated me," sighed one lady who'd consumed fifteen banana daiquiris and was laid out on top of the bar. "That's why I drink," she explained before passing out.

This reporter left the Dew Drop Inn with a greater understanding of the plight of the single woman and a bar tab like you wouldn't believe.

But these observations are not a reason for single women to despair; they are the reason for them to persevere.

From Adam's first "date" with Eve to the courtship of Madonna and Sean, dating has always been a test of personal endurance. And it always will be because, as the sign above the bar at the Dew Drop Inn read: If God meant life to be easy for singles, why did He create New Year's Eve?

Dating for Fun and Profit: A Financial Overview

Dating is probably the most important aspect of a single person's life. A huge amount of time, effort, and money is invested in dating, yet very little planning is applied to this crucial area of life.

In our professional lives, we spend an extraordinary amount

of energy developing plans to achieve our projected goals. We are a generation who worships at the MBA shrine. We believe in cost projections and profit-and-loss statements. So, why haven't we applied these basic techniques to our social lives?

When was the last time you sat down and charted a business plan for your dating career? When was the last time you tabulated your cost-per-unit date? When was the last time you inventoried your backlist of social engagements? If your answer is, "I don't have the foggiest idea what that means," then this section is for you.

Here is where you'll learn to chart your social life, to prepare a business plan for your dating career, and to analyze a potential date's assets and debits. You'll establish a profit center for your social life and learn how to depreciate your last boyfriend as easily as your car.

This may be the most important chapter you'll ever read, so pay attention. If you need to go the bathroom, then do it now.

Dating Business Plan

The Marketplace

According to *Dating Industry Trends*, a professional magazine covering the singles market, up until the late 1960s dating was a routine activity involving cars, rock 'n' roll, and poodle skirts. Today, dating is more complicated.

Kirby Denver, editor of *Dating Trends*, says: "We describe dating in the 1980s as being like the classic Roller Derby, a life-threatening contest to determine who will get dumped first."

While socializing is more extensive today than ever before,

dating is experiencing a downward spiral in some respects. *Dating Trends* has predicted that from 1989 to 1992, the incidence of dating will increase 10 percent in units and 47 percent in dollars, while decreasing 97 percent in personal satisfaction. The increased population will account for the rise in units, inflation will account for the rise in dollars, and bad press about various social diseases will account for the decrease in satisfaction.

Who is affected by this trend? The market for dating has traditionally been generalized as the "under thirty-five" age group. This is due to several factors. Historically, people over thirty-five have been thought to be too smart to still be dating. Prior dating experience in high school, college, and in the workplace was considered enough to encourage most people to marry the first person who'd consent to have them.

Because of this, most rational thinkers projected the demise of dating. Yet, for the past three decades, dating has continued despite the fact that birth control pills cause cancer, herpes is incurable, and there's not a single humorous remark anyone can make about AIDS. Still, dating continues to prosper. This leads most experts to conclude:

1. People are either incredibly stupid or unbelievably horny.
2. The staying power of dating is beyond the scope of rational thinking. According to Dr. Donald Rumbacon, a physicist with the Arkansas Atomic Energy Commission, "We have projected that the only things to survive a nuclear holocaust will be the household cockroach and the blind date."

Frequency

Every weekday in this country, there are approximately 37,895,987 dates. Of this figure, approximately 22,456,789 are complete bummers. While this leaves 15,439,198 so-called successful dates, none of them happen to me—or to the people I hang out with.

During any given week, these numbers remain relatively constant from Tuesday to Friday. The number of dates drops radically, however, on Saturday, when most married men return home to their wives.

Conversely, the number of blind dates and first dates increases on Saturday night as single women attempt to make their married boyfriends jealous.

Sunday night dates, while numerous, appear to end early, usually before dark, because, no matter how old or sophisticated a person gets, they always think of Sunday as a "school night."

According to the latest government census, Monday nights everyone stays home to watch *Monday Night Football* or *Kate and Allie*.

Dating Spread Sheet: Breakdown by Type of Date

	Jan.	Feb.	March	April
Blind dates				
First dates				
Married men dated				
Younger men dated				
Dating disasters				
Pickups/One-night stands				
Affairs (more than 1 date)				
Relationships (more than 2 dates)				
TOTAL DATES PER MONTH				

Inventory and Backlist

The strength of any business rests in its backlist and inventory, and the same is true for your social life. Dr. Marcia Quisont, a Ph.D. in Manic Datology (the study of dating patterns among depressed singles) at Columbia University, has developed a backlist spread sheet that the layperson can use to inventory her social warehouse.

Comments

1. In terms of units, this spread sheet can help you determine your most heavily dated months. Think about why you were so popular during that particular time frame. Were you wearing anything new? A new haircut? Were you frequenting a new singles bar? Doing drugs?

2. If the number zero (0) crops up more than thirty-nine times in this chart, you need to increase your monthly unit dates. You are obviously not getting out enough.

3. If you are heavy in the pick-ups/one-night-stands col-

May	June	July	Aug.	Sept.	Oct.	Nov.	Dec.

umn, but weak in first dates, then you may want to reassess your criteria for selecting a guy to escort you home.

4. If you are heavy in the blind dates column but weak on affairs or relationships, you need a better set of friends fixing you up.

5. If your only completed category is dating disasters, you need *Jane Fonda's Workout* book, record, and tape.

Advertising and Promotion

One way to increase your number of unit dates is to concentrate on marketing and selling your product (namely, yourself). You may need to invest in advertising space to promote yourself and your wares to the general male public. You should not be embarrassed or dismiss this idea out of hand. One of the major themes of dating in the 1980s is clear to anyone who reads magazines: It pays to advertise.

In almost every publication from *New York* magazine to *Stench: The Trade Magazine of the Dead Fish Industry*, singles ads are the largest growing area of advertising revenue. Pretty soon these magazines will be 90 percent singles ads and only 10 percent feature stories and cigarette ads.

Unfortunately, this glut of advertising greatly decreases your chance of meeting anyone. With so much competition in the singles ad field, you need to be more original.

Use your imagination. For instance, the perfect place to advertise is your car. Get in on the "Baby on Board" placard fad. Use your back window to declare "Single on Board" or "Dateless on Board."

Get a car phone and plaster your number on the back window. Or you get your phone number on a vanity license plate: 555-5555.

Post bumper stickers that declare: I BRAKE FOR SINGLE
WOMEN; I BRAKE FOR CUTE GUYS; I'D RATHER BE ON A DATE; I
BLIND DATE, DO YOU?; HONK IF YOU'RE FREE FOR DINNER!

If you don't own a car, use any of these clever slogans in
your own original way—on a T-shirt or baseball hat, or tat-
tooed on your forehead. Wear a sandwich board or, if you live
in a high-rent district, a croissant board.

If you can afford it, rent a billboard. Hire a skywriter. If it
pays to advertise, remember it pays even more to advertise
big!

Profit and Loss

Advertising dollars are only one of the factors you will need
to consider when calculating your dating revenue. Naturally,
a profitable social life begins with a reliable budget. To project a budget for the coming year, you need to tabulate your
cost-per-unit date.

Your cost-per-unit date will vary according to such factors
as how much your new hair mousse cost, whether you chose
that collagen mask during this month's facial, and if you ever
again wear that red lace bra you bought especially for a hot
date. Using the following flow chart, you can tally the total
amount invested on any particular date. Calculating your dating debits will help you decide if the money spent was worth
the investment. According to a reliable yuppie, "Your cost-
per-unit date is your most reliable guideline in determining
whether or not it pays to continue dating that certain guy."

Cost-per-Unit Date Flow Chart

Dollar Amount	TOM	DICK	HARRY
SELF:			
Clothes (include undergarments)			
Hair			
Shoes			
Makeup (other cosmetics)			
Bleach (hair, mustache, etc.)			
Dry-cleaning bills			
Manicure/Pedicure			
Fashion accessories			
HAIR:			
Cut			
Equipment (dryer, hot rollers, etc.)			
Products (mousse, gels, sprays, etc.)			
Utensils (barettes, bows, etc.)			
APARTMENT/HOUSE			
Food and drink			
Maid fee			
Laundry (sheets, towels, etc.)			
ENTERTAINMENT			
Tickets (movie, concert, etc.)			
Restaurant bill			
Bar tab			

Cost-per-Unit Date Flow Chart

Dollar Amount	TOM	DICK	HARRY
SUPPLIES			
Ajax (for bathroom)			
Contraceptive jelly/ condoms (per gross)			
RESEARCH			
Magazines (for fashion ideas)			
TRANSPORTATION			
Car ($0.14 per mile)			
Gas, tolls			
Subway fare			
MISCELLANEOUS			
Phone bill			
Marital aids			
Valium or other drugs			
Diet food (previous to date)			
TOTAL DOLLAR AMOUNTS			

Formula

Once you have assessed the amount you spent on each particular date, you can easily calculate your cost-per-unit date. The formula is simple:

Total dollar amount ÷ Number of dates = Cost-per-unit date

For example, if you spent a total of $450 on Tom and dated him five times, figure:

$450 ÷ 5 = $90 per unit date.

If, on the other hand, you spent $450 on Dick but only dated him twice, your unit cost would be much higher:

$450 ÷ 2 = $225 per unit date.

Now, ask yourself, given the cost of Donna Karan in today's marketplace, was Dick worth $135 more *per date* than Tom?

Comments

1. When calculating cost-per-unit date, take into account that none of these expenditures are tax deductible, although they really should be. This means that the money costs you even more than you think, a concept I never fully grasped but one that seems to enrage most accountants.
2. While the cost-per-unit date is an essential tool in today's dating market, it is not the only guideline to use. A very high cost-per-unit date can be mitigated by the following two factors:

   - Expensive gifts. For instance in the above example, if Dick bought you an expensive gold watch for your birthday, you can throw these calculations out the window, along with Tom.
   - Great sex. If he's good in bed, he's worth every dime he costs you, and then some.

Contracts

While your standard dating contract will cover the financial obligations of both parties, it is wise to be quite specific as to who will get custody of any property remaining after the first date (especially in the event that there is no second date).

Any leftover brandy, for instance, should remain the possession of the person at whose home it was poured.

Also, be careful with your option clause. You don't want to obligate yourself to a second date before completing the first date. Make sure your lawyer negotiates a thirty-day grace period so that you can change your identity, if necessary, before fulfilling your obligation to date the guy again.

Research and Development

R&D is money you invest (often called venture capital) when your social life needs a complete overhaul. This can include a week at the Golden Door Spa in California or a session with a new therapist. Venture capital is used to discover if there's a new and datable person underneath your current personality.

Return Policy

All dates are returnable, no matter what he tells you.

Subsidiary Rights

Any income derived from selling material based on your date is the sole property of the person making the sale.

Conclusions

Strengths
   a) Your social life is repairable.
   b) You have good genes and clean underwear.
   c) You are basically a nice person.
   d) Your cat likes you.

Weaknesses

a) Your social life is costing you too much money.
b) You need to date more.
c) Your gums bleed.

Goals

a) Increase the number of dates.
b) Decrease your cost-per-unit date.
c) Get married, have a baby, live happily ever after.

Pre-
paring to
Date

 I only like two kinds of men: domestic and imported.

—*Mae West*

Princess with Great Hopes Kissing the Local Frog.

Stine

How Desperate Are You?

Being dateless for an extended period of time can seriously (perhaps permanently) warp your ideals. You may experience a considerable drop in your expectations. You may pass from merely "hoping to meet the right man" into the dreaded psychotic state known to therapists as Dateless and Desperate (D&D).

Shrinks use the following question to test a patient's tendency to become hopelessly D&D. Read the story below carefully, putting yourself in this situation. Be sure to answer as openly and honestly as possible.

Dateless and Desperate (D&D) Test

You meet a handsome man in the vegetable department of your local grocery. He asks for your help in selecting a ripe cantaloupe. You notice he is not wearing a wedding ring.

While you squeeze or sniff the fruit (depending on the method your mother taught you), you ask if he's new to the neighborhood.

"Not exactly," he replies. "I've sort of been out of town for the last few years."

33

"On business?" you ask, noticing his finely developed shoulders.

"Yeah, sort of," he sheepishly replies. "I've been in prison."

"Prison? Like, in jail?"

"Yeah," he says. "I murdered my wife, sort of."

What Is Your Immediate Response?

a) You drop the melon, scream for help, and run like hell.

b) You hand the melon to the ex-con and quietly slink away from him.

c) You blink once and say, "Oh? Does that mean you're single?"

Score

If you answered (a), you are obviously desperate for attention. No one screams in the produce department without causing general havoc to the more delicate fruits. You need sexual satisfaction to calm your nerves. You are in the gravest danger of becoming a victim of the dreaded D&D syndrome.

A classic example of D&D, often cited by psychiatrists, is the case of poor Daisy Singer, a young woman who, in high school, was voted Most Likely to Live in New Jersey. Daisy's condition went generally unnoticed and untreated until the day she filled out a job application for a position as an assistant executive secretary for a major corporation.

When asked, *Are you married?*, Daisy wrote:

"No, but I'm not without a companion. For the past six years I've been dating my television or, as I like to tease myself, Romancing the Sony (ha-ha!).

"I see Sony almost every night. We share the laughter, the cheers, the news, the embarrassment of hemorrhoidal itch. In short, Sony lights up my life.

"Oh, I've had lots of boyfriends, but none were as loyal as Sony—or as easy to satisfy. To turn on my Sony, all I have to do is press a button, which is sure a lot easier than having to wear spike heels and a leather garter belt to bed."

The company psychiatrist who reviewed Daisy's application asked her to explain her lengthy response.

"Gee," Daisy replied, "I thought it was an essay question."

Fortunately, Daisy found help. She's been in treatment for the past five years and can now almost get through an entire date without humming a commercial jingle every few minutes.

Daisy's inspiring tale should serve to remind all of us that early detection is our best defense in the war against D&D.

Women Who Self-Help Too Much

It is a well-established fact that women prone to becoming Dateless and Desperate (D&D) are generally intelligent and well-read. Interested in improving their lot in life, these women work extremely hard to keep up with the current body of work in the self-help field. The problem is that the anxiety and fear of becoming D&D is often so great that these women become self-help-aholics. Known as a disease of denial, the self-help-aholic is totally obsessed with books of pop psychology.

The disease starts slowly with one self-help book a month, then escalates to two a month, then three, four, five and so on. Before too long, these women cannot leave the house without a paperback book clutched in each hand.

The disease is difficult to cure because so much reading distorts the addict's sense of perception about the world and gives her the feeling that any problem can be solved as long as it's listed in the index.

The self-help-aholic quickly becomes the self-help-hypochondriac, absorbing into her personality every symptom detailed on the back jackets of these books. This is when she is in serious danger of overimproving herself.

The following chart is a sampling of some of the symptoms of this insidious addiction. To test your own susceptibility to the disease, carefully review the listing of psychological conditions and check off any that you feel apply to you.

Instant Self-Analysis Menu

Column A	*Column B*
A smart woman making foolish choices	A woman who thinks she's nothing without a man
A woman who loves too much	A successful woman stuck to an angry man
A smart cookie, crumbled	
A woman who loves men who hate women	A woman who plays Wendy to Peter Pan
A woman men love; a woman men leave	A woman who gives up herself to be loved by him

SCORE

Select	To get diagnosed
One from Column A or B	Mildly paranoid
One from A & One from B	Lacking self-esteem
Two from A & One from B	Medium paranoid
Two from A & Two from B	Without any esteem
Three from A & Two from B	Paranoid and depressed
Four from A & Three from B	Comes with egg roll
All of the above	A woman who reads too much

If you understand even part of this chart, clearly you have spent too much time reading self-help books and thinking about what's wrong with you. Your mind has been hopelessly warped by Phil Donahue, Oprah Winfrey, and Jane Pauley. You are over-self-helped.

Granted it is very difficult to be single in a self-help world. You are an easy prey to the psychobabble of the so-called experts who write books about women's problems. You're confused and you want an easy answer. You're upset because none of these books have actually changed your life. You're distraught because you don't have a date for your cousin Debbie's wedding.

Quite simply, you are suffering from what psychologist Dr. Daniel Killjoy calls *The Toto Dilemma*.

As explained by Dr. Killjoy: "The Toto Dilemma is when women allow men, particularly handsome male authors like myself, to treat them like dogs. You put a good-looking guy like me on Donahue and all I have to do is say, 'Fetch,' and women flock to the bookstores for my book. Women today are in serious danger of turning self-help into self-destruct. That's why I wrote my book—to cash in on this situation."

Unlike most of the popular self-help books cited in the Instant Self-Analysis Menu, Dr. Killjoy's recently published book, *The Toto Dilemma: When Authors Treat You Like Dogs!*, does not claim to have the answer for achieving inner peace. In fact, Dr. Killjoy seriously doubts the existence of such a phenomenon. In his opening paragraph, he quotes the philosopher and fashion sage Fran Lebowitz, who said: "There is no such thing as inner peace. There's only nervousness and death."

Dr. Killjoy's thesis also differs radically from other popular self-help books in that he does not put a lot of emphasis on self-esteem. "Self-esteem has become the microwave oven of the pop psychology field, everyone's got to have it. I wonder why?" he asks in the first chapter, entitled *I'd Divorce Myself, If I Could*. "There's only three things you basically need to improve your life: (1) a good hair colorist; (2) a summer house; and (3) to get laid."

To this end, Dr. Killjoy recommends that you immediately stop reading other people's self-help books and concentrate solely on his book. "We're not in Kansas anymore," says the doctor. "We must prepare ourselves to enter the dating market."

The Toto Dilemma is loaded with down-to-earth advice for successful dating. For example, Dr. Killjoy recommends that you avoid materialistic considerations and be more realistic when dating a man for the first time. "Remember it's not how much money your date spends on you that counts," writes Dr. Killjoy. "What really matters is how well he dresses."

His advice is to avoid jeopardizing your first date by living in the future and to try not to be concerned with security. As Dr. Killjoy points out: "You can never fully own another human being, although sometimes you can rent with an option to buy."

The Toto Dilemma shows you how to get out of your self-imposed doghouse by teaching you the following:

- Where your extra erogenous zones are located and whether you have to pay a toll to get to them.

- Why, when you are good, you are very, very good, but when you are bad, you date more.

- How to lie down and roll over, along with 167 other ways to say I love you.

- Why your two most compatible astrology signs are Slim and None.

"Do not go gentle into Saturday night," advises Dr. Killjoy. "With *The Toto Dilemma*, you can join the mass of women leading lives of noisy desperation."

Learning to Compromise: A Personal Note

Before we delve into the specifics of getting and keeping a date, I wanted to interject a personal note about the fine art of compromising.

Now, this comes from a woman who was raised to believe that I'd never have to settle for less than my ideal.

My mother always told me that there were plenty of fish in the sea and that somewhere out there was the man of my dreams.

Of course, one must take into account the fundamental difference between dating in Mom's day and in mine. In my mother's time, it was a shock to hear a man say, "Frankly, my dear, I don't give a damn." Today, it's a surprise when a date doesn't say it.

Still, I had my standards and, of course, I was young enough to believe my mother knew what she was talking about when she said, "There's a lid for every pot."

Consequently, over the years, I developed and refined a long list of everything I wanted in a mate. Here's what my perfect "lid" would be like:

He should be tall, dark, and handsome (of course); rich, famous, and successful; thoughtful, romantic, sensitive, gentle, and good-natured. He should excel at sports and be kind to animals, relatives, and me. He had to love kids, my funny smile, and walks by the beach. He should be a good dancer, if not a great one, and it was essential that he know how to dress. No part of his person should smell bad.

It was a definite negative if he was fond of contact sports, but, in all fairness, I supposed that I could learn to adapt to the occasional football game on Sunday afternoon, as long as it didn't interfere with our weekend visits to my mom.

From this list, you might not be surprised to learn that I never married.

Well, times have changed.

I've gotten older. Much older. I eventually had to acknowledge that maybe I was being a little too choosy. After several years, and $26,000 in therapy, I am now more realistic.

I've refined my requirements somewhat. Now I'm looking for a man who holds down a steady job and isn't carrying an infectious disease.

And, frankly, if he has trouble making a living, well, I can accept that. I suppose, with my successful career, I could support both of us; but I'm real firm on the disease part, at least I think I am.

Actually, I exaggerate. I haven't abandoned *all* my standards. I do have two absolute requirements. I will not go out with a man who wears more jewelry than me, and I'll never, ever go to bed with a guy who calls me Babe. Other than that, however, I'm real flexible.

One of the more fundamental truths about dating is that you can learn more from Sophie Tucker than from your own mother. Sophie once said: "From birth to age 18, a girl needs good parents, from 18 to 35 she needs good looks, from 35 to 55 she needs a good personality, and from 55 on she needs cash."

Sophie Tucker was one really together lady. I wish I knew the name of her therapist.

How to Get a Date

 She who hesitates is not only lost but miles from the next exit.

—*Unknown*

Places to Meet Men

You do not need to be a dating genius to know you cannot start dating without first meeting. Meeting is, in fact, the crucial first step in the dating process.

In olden times, men and women had it easy. When they were ready to start dating, their parents contacted the local matchmaker, who selected an appropriate candidate and arranged for the first date. (This worked well because no one had an answering machine in those days.)

The purpose of these arranged meetings was marriage, and, with a big enough dowry, most women could count on getting married or, at the very least, asked out a second time. Not a bad arrangement, if you ask me.

Matchmaking has been much maligned in this century, mainly due to the advent of video dating, and is all but lost to us as an art form. This is unfortunate, especially for women with trust funds. However, as my Nana Sunshine would say, there's no use crying over spilt milk. Those days are long gone, and now we're left to our own devices.

Let's face it, it's not easy to meet men because it's not easy to *find* them.

The key is knowing where to look.

45

Bars

Of course, the most obvious place is your neighborhood bar. You don't need to watch Miller beer commercials to know how much men like to drink. But you can substantially increase your odds of meeting a man by knowing the best time to hit the bars. You can find this out by checking your *TV Guide* for listings of major sports events. If you don't know all that much about sports (and what single woman really does?), be advised to look for events that include the following words: *Playoff, Series,* or *Bowl.* Pay particular attention when these words are aggrandized, as in *World* Series or *Super* Bowl. The more adjectives they add to these events, the better.

Remember, during this time, only to frequent bars with television sets. In fact, you can pretty much ratio the size of the TV screen to the number of men in attendance (i.e., the bigger the screen, the bigger the crowd). Hit Madison Square Garden during one of those closed circuit boxing events and you might fill your social calendar for a month.

Arrive at your selected establishment several hours before the event takes place so that you're assured a well-positioned bar stool. That way, if you don't meet anyone special, you can sell your seat when you leave.

Co-op Meetings

If you're interested in meeting a yuppy, then you'd be wise to attend as many co-op meetings as possible but never in your own building. You don't ever want to date one of your neighbors because you'll never again be able to do your laundry in the basement without first putting on makeup and deodorant. Who needs that kind of aggravation? No, you should only attend co-op meetings in buildings other than your own. Ask your friends to invite you to their annual meetings (and remember to reciprocate the favor).

If your friends tell you their meetings are "closed to the public," they may be keeping these social events to themselves, so you'll need to be more inventive (and to find new friends). You can find out when a particular building is holding a shareholders meeting by scanning the bulletin boards in apartment house lobbies or by bribing the doormen. (Check with your accountant—such "tips" are probably deductible from your income tax.)

If you don't own a co-op, you should try even harder to meet a man who does. As your mother would say, it's just as easy to fall in love with a man who owns real estate as it is to fall in love with one who rents.

Reunions

I have recently discovered that high school reunions are excellent places to meet men. In general, people only attend their reunion if they've achieved a relative measure of success in life and if they're looking for a date. But, be forewarned, the same rules apply here as in co-op meetings. Go to anyone else's reunion but your own. At your own high school reunion you'll only be reminded of what the man shortage means to you; namely, that guys you wouldn't let near your locker in high school are now snubbing you. This is not a lesson you need to learn more than once.

Off-Track Betting (OTB)

If you're not too choosy, you might want to check out OTB or make a quick tour of your local racetrack. Betting establishments attract men like flies to honey, and, as I said, if you're not particular about dating certain species of insects, OTB may be the place for you.

The Pipeline

If you're willing to travel, or just super-desperate, the best place in the world to meet unattached men is on the Alaska pipeline. I'm told that the trek through the frozen tundra is well worth the effort for any woman who wants to know what it feels like to be Victoria Principal.

Police Stations and Firehouses

Getting arrested is a great way to meet a good-looking cop. Remember, too, that policemen, like firemen, are accustomed to making house calls. A minor fire or an imagined robbery can fill your living room with handsome men in uniform.

Emergency Rooms

Overdose, very carefully, after making arrangements for a good friend to come calling no more than seven seconds after you ingest your drug of choice. In the ambulance, or at the hospital, give your card to all doctors, residents, male nurses, or other personnel who look like potential dating material.

Miscellaneous

Group therapy meetings and bankruptcy court are good places for finding desperate (i.e., vulnerable) men.

Other places to meet men include pool halls, construction sites, military installations, Boy Scout meetings, porno movie houses, steam rooms, prisons, ballparks, and the men's department of Bloomingdale's, if you have the energy.

There is an alternative to going out and finding a man—which brings us to the horrific blind date.

The Woman Who Mistook Her Blind Date for a Potential Husband

Everyone knows that the best policy is to not expect miracles from life. "I didn't want to be rich," Kate (Mrs. Zero) Mostel once claimed, "I just wanted enough to get the couch reupholstered."

Still, when you go out on a blind date, it's hard not to entertain the following fantasy:

The doorbell rings. You get up from your dressing table, take one last lingering look at yourself in the mirror, and nod with approval. You open the front door.

He stands in the doorway, but you can barely see his face behind all of those enormous yellow roses he's holding in his hands. He presents you with the bouquet.

He is incredibly tall and looks like a cross between William Hurt, Tom Cruise, and the guy you loved madly in sixth grade.

His crooked smile reveals his vulnerability, a great set of real white teeth, and a neat dimple in his left cheek.

He is rendered speechless by your beauty and falls instantly in love with you.

The next day, you discover he is a millionaire brain surgeon/

criminal lawyer who pilots his own Lear jet and owns an oceanfront summer house in Southampton.

Say hello to your dream blind date.

Say good-bye to reality.

The blind date is genuine proof that truth is stranger than fiction. The facts speak for themselves:

A perfect stranger calls you up. You have an extremely uncomfortable conversation, which you both pretend to enjoy. He asks you to see a movie that you have no interest in seeing. You worry about what to wear, what he'll look like, and whether you'll have anything to talk to him about.

In your heart of hearts, you know you will have a terrible time, the date will be a total washout. But, still, you have an anxiety attack if your hair frizzes while you are getting ready for him to arrive.

Your tendency during this initial stage of anxiety is to curse the friend or relative responsible for arranging the date. Try to avoid hating this person.

It is best to remember that the people who set you up on a blind date have the best of intentions, really they do. You need to keep this in mind, because the truth is you can never, never believe what anyone tells you when they describe the person you are being fixed up with.

If you're told, for instance, that your blind date looks like a movie star; you're not told that the movie star is Meat Loaf.

If you're told that your blind date is a great catch, you're not told that his wife's alimony lawyer has been trying to catch the guy for months.

If you're told this is a match made in heaven; you're not told it was on an off-day.

If you're told your blind date is an old-fashioned guy, you're not told that this applies mainly to his clothes.

But, hey! You're single, and although your phone rings constantly, it's always your mother calling you.

It is a well-known fact, by the way, that the worst blind dates, bar none, are those arranged by your mother. It doesn't matter whether the guy is a district attorney, a genius, a best-selling writer. If your mother found him, he's a geek.

Regardless, you want to take advantage of every opportunity, so you accept blind date after blind date. Eventually, however, your inner psyche begins to rebel.

Your cousin Rhonda offers to fix you up with her brother's accountant, but instead you choose to stay home and watch *St. Elsewhere*.

Your best friend meets a great new guy and you forget to ask: Does he have any single friends?

You make a firm decision that blind dating is not for you. You begin to consider the alternatives: celibacy or surrogate dating.

An Alternative to Blind Dates: Surrogate Dating

Until recently (March 16, 1986, to be specific), single people didn't have much of an alternative to blind dating. A blind date was something you suffered through in order to tell yourself you were doing everything possible to enhance your social life. As we all know, everything changed with the advent of surrogate dating.

Surrogate dating, the practice of hiring a substitute person to date for you, was inadvertently invented by Mindy Wonger, a thirty-nine-year-old stenographer from Pasadena, California. Mindy, single and sorry, answered the phone one day and found herself accepting a blind date from Dave, an acquaintance of Mindy's Al-Anon qualifier.

After hanging up the phone, Mindy realized she'd rather walk barefoot on a bed of glass than go on another blind date, yet she was afraid to cancel the date with Dave. Except for her nightly Al-Anon meetings, Mindy hadn't gone out in three months, and, as every single woman knows, opportunity doesn't knock all that often after you've been diagnosed as a Woman Who Loves Too Much.

Mindy solved her problem by hiring her roommate, Carla, to date Dave. In exchange for not having to clean the bathroom for two weeks, Carla agreed to masquerade as Mindy and to have dinner with Dave. Carla wore a wig and Mindy's Liz Claiborne jumpsuit. Carla also promised not to fall in love and to return Dave to Mindy in the event he proved to be marriage material.

Thus, the first surrogate dating arrangement was made.

Today, surrogate dating is a bit more complex, since not everyone has a roommate who looks good in Liz Claiborne. Agencies such as The Next Best Thing in Atlanta have been established to match clients and surrogate dates. Prospective clients can select surrogates with the same hair color and body type. Just like You in Jacksonville, Florida, organizes their employee surrogate pool into nine basic personality categories. Clients can decide for themselves which "type" best matches their personality and can choose from the following classifications: Princess, Workaholic, Hippie, Easily Addicted, Punk, Sex Symbol, Homebody, Artist, and Adaptable.

Fees up to two thousand dollars have been paid, especially when the date has been arranged through the parents of either of the parties involved. And, because money is now involved, written contracts are not uncommon.

Surrogate contracts specify such contingencies as additional bonus payments to rehire the surrogate for the couple's first fight or for their first "totally honest" discussion about previous sexual encounters, whichever comes first.

Surrogate dating has drastically reduced blind dating and, up until recently, was considered a boon for the singles market. In late 1986, Club Med established a Club Surrogate on St. Luigi's Island where guys and gals who were too shy to travel alone could hire a surrogate to vacation for them while they stayed home and watched television. An episode of *Family Ties* features Michael J. Fox on a surrogate date. *People* magazine interviewed five surrogate singles for their September 23, 1986, issue. In late fall of the same year, Tama Janowitz published a hip novel about the New York surrogate dating scene.

Then, suddenly, surrogate dating was nearly brought to a screeching halt by Mary Beth Whiteface and Elysse Sterp in their now legendary lawsuit, *Sterp* v. *Whiteface*.

The shocking case began in April of 1986, when Mary Beth Whiteface was hired by Elysse Sterp to date Marvin Slavin, a nephew of Ms. Sterp's mother's canasta partner. Mary Beth was paid ten thousand dollars, full combat pay, because the date involved not only Ms. Sterp's mother but her mother's canasta partner, who was also a second cousin and a bigmouth like you wouldn't believe.

Although Mary Beth claimed she only took the job out of pity for the dateless Elysse, lawyers for Ms. Sterp maintained it was no coincidence that in March of 1986, Mary Beth suffered a serious shopping attack in Bloomingdale's, specifically in the Giorgio Armani department, and desperately needed the cash.

Whatever her motives, and much to her surprise, Mary Beth enjoyed her date with Marvin. In fact, she had such a good time, she decided to keep Marvin all to herself.

In complete violation of her contract with Elysse, Mary Beth introduced Marvin to her parents.

In testimony to the court, Mary Beth later explained, "Your Honor, it was just one of those things, one of those crazy flings."

"A trip to the moon on gossamer wings?" prompted Ms. Whiteface's lawyer.

"Just one of those things," sighed Mary Beth, choking back her tears.

"One of those bells that now and then rings, I suppose," scoffed Elysse Sterp.

The most damaging argument the clever district attorney used against Mary Beth was the fact she'd neglected to tell Elysse that, on their first date, Mary Beth and Marvin engaged in a long walk by the ocean while Marvin recited his favorite lines from Woody Allen movies. (Beach walks are absolutely forbidden during surrogate dating. In fact, the rules of surrogate dating discourage encounters near any body of water, including lakes, streams, rivers, indoor pools, and Jacuzzis. Especially Jacuzzis.)

Almost as damning, Mary Beth and Marvin ran off for the weekend to the mountains. From Ye Olde Country Inn in Connecticut, Mary Beth called Elysse and pleaded to be released from her contract. When Elysse refused, Mary Beth threatened to tell Marvin that Elysse had herpes.

After a long and arduous court battle, the judge decided in favor of Elysse Sterp, requiring Mary Beth Whiteface to honor her contractual obligation and to release Marvin Slavin from the Whiteface cellar. The judge further instructed Mary Beth to return Marvin's ID bracelet.

In Mary Beth's favor, the judge ruled that Marvin and Mary Beth could maintain non-weekend visitation rights, but only if they went Dutch treat.

The Whiteface/Sterp case has, of course, raised many complex questions about the moral and ethical basis for surrogate dating.

- Even though we have the technology to provide everyone with a surrogate date, do we have any moral obligation to be truthful with the people we date?

- Does Mary Beth Whiteface have the right to fall in love and abandon her contractual obligations?

- Does Elysse Sterp really have herpes?

The adverse publicity of the Whiteface/Sterp case has greatly decreased the practice of surrogate dating. Always controversial, surrogate dating is now even more opposed by conservatives, born-agains, krishnas, and most married people in general. The only groups still supporting surrogate dating are lawyers and a splinter group of radical feminists who feel women should have the legal right to do anything.

In spite of any opposition, however, surrogate dating is unlikely to go away. Anyone who has ever accepted a blind date because they needed to meet someone new knows that no price is too high to pay when contemplating the pain and agony of opening the front door on a complete stranger who, in all probability, has dandruff.

How to Call a Man for a Date

Unfortunately, women like myself (broadly speaking, all females over the age of eighteen) are at a great disadvantage in today's dating marketplace. In our day (specifically the 1950s, 1960s, and even parts of the 1970s), only the guys had the privilege of choosing a prospective date and doing the asking. For girls, there was only one method for getting a date. You waited by your telephone for a guy to call. If he didn't call, you washed your hair.

Okay, so maybe it wasn't the most dynamic way to build a social life. In our defense, it was all we knew, never having been properly trained in the guerrilla dating tactics of today. (This is not our fault. Like most things that go wrong in our lives, we can blame our mothers for not adequately advising us.) Also, we didn't have Princess Stephanie or Cyndi Lauper as role models. Those of us who grew up with Annette, *Sonny and Cher*, or Mary Tyler Moore may not have dated very much, but we had our dignity, our self-respect, our pride, and, for sure, we had clean hair.

Well, times have changed. Calling a guy for a date is as common today as Korean salad bars. Girls no longer stand on ceremony, and we older women need to adapt to these new ways. The 1980s demand aggression, guts, and lots of attitude. Women today must toss themselves into the dating pool, whether or not they wear a life preserver. Dating in the 1980s means: Sink or Swim!

The advantages of asking a man for a date are twofold. By making that call, you are taking control of your social life while at the same time gaining a unique opportunity to experience the heady power that comes from freedom of choice.

Calling a man for a date is a lot like learning how to insert a diaphragm; the first time is really embarrassing, but once you get used to the mess, you'll find the long-range advantages outweigh your initial repulsion.

If you are nervous about calling that cute guy you met in the Xerox shop, here are some useful suggestions to help build up your confidence.

You begin by convincing yourself to make that call. Stand in front of your bathroom mirror and tell yourself that you *will* call him. Persuade yourself that you actually *want* to call him, you *need* to call him. Concentrate on your image in the mirror. Remind yourself that this is not the face of a coward. Stare long and hard at yourself. (Warning: Do not get sidetracked into attacking any facial blemishes or bleaching some section of hair above your shoulders.)

If you are particularly nervous, it sometimes helps if you prepare for the worst-case scenario. A technique I often use when confronted with a difficult situation is to ask myself: *What's the worst possible thing that could happen?*

When I decided to call Darrell, a handsome man I'd taken

home from a party one gloriously naughty evening, I asked myself this: What will happen if I call him?

I came up with the following list of possibilities:

a) He'll say yes.
b) He'll say no, but thank me for calling.
c) He'll say no, he can't go out with me because he forgot to mention he was attached to his wife, someone else's wife, a girlfriend, or a really weird pet.
d) He'll tell me to never call him again.

I prepared myself for each of the above contingencies. Whatever answer he gave, I was ready with a witty reply. I felt confident enough to make that phone call.

Just like a man, Darrell defied my list of possibilities, coming up with a scenario that was far beyond my imagination: Darrell didn't remember who I was. "I don't think I ever got your name," was the way Darrell explained his reaction.

My therapist artfully tried to comfort me. "At least you know the reason *why* Darrell hasn't called," Dr. Yesandno said, not unkindly.

"Yeah," I mumbled, "I suppose it's hard to call someone when you don't know their last name."

"Or their first name," my therapist, a real stickler for details, pointed out.

I waited six months before I called another male, other than Dr. Yesandno, of course.

I did, however, use the time productively by practicing my dialing skill. Every day I made at least two phony phone calls, pretending each time that I was calling Darrell. My therapist wondered why I wasn't arrested for public obscenity, even though I explained that most of the men I called seemed to actually enjoy my profanities.

Those phony phone calls taught me that practice was essential in order to "give good phone." Telephone technique is an acquired skill. By the time I was ready to call another man for a date, I had the confidence to forge ahead.

Since those early years, I have established a working routine that helps me overcome my shyness.

If you feel insecure about calling that special guy, try the following Nine Step Program that I have developed. It works for me, maybe it'll work for you!

1. Drink a glass of wine, quickly.
2. Clutch teddy bear to your chest.
3. Practice what you are going to say by talking to your teddy bear.
4. Pick up the phone and place it in your lap. Take several deep breaths.
5. Carry phone and teddy bear to dining room table.
6. Crawl under table.
7. Grit teeth, hold breath, squeeze eyes shut, and pray.
8. Dial.
9. When a woman answers the phone, hang up.

While this routine works really well for me, there are several other methods that I have also tried, with varying degrees of success. If you are not comfortable calling him from your home, call him from a party or during another date. Make sure there is plenty of noise in the background. Pretend you are so busy this was the only free moment you had to call him.

Call him in the middle of the night. If you wake him from a deep sleep, you may catch him at a weak moment when he's likely to say yes to just about anything.

Whichever method you choose, try not to panic during those excruciating moments after dialing but before the phone is answered, when "rrringg!" is the loneliest sound that you'll ever hear.

Keep an airsickness bag handy if you tend to panic under pressure.

These moments will be among the longest and most stressful of your life. Your instinct will be to hang up, which you will probably do a few times before you are steady enough to allow him time to answer the phone.

The standard procedure, if you've called and then hung up, is to wait fifteen minutes before attempting to call again.

If, however, you've called, he's answered, and then you've hung up, the standard procedure is call back immediately and say that your phone is broken.

Between attempts to reach him, boost your own morale by reminding yourself how brave you are and what a good thing you are doing. With a little bit of initiative, he will answer, say he's busy for the next six months, and you will be well on your way to your next major heartbreak.

Calling a man for a date is a real life experience; one that all women should try at least once.

So, get out there with your File-O-Fax phone sections and call him for a date!

If you can't do it for yourself, then do it for the cause.

As women, we need to fight for the right to determine our dating destiny. What our feminist forepersons achieved for us in the boardrooms, we will now achieve in the bedroom.

As we move closer and closer to a nonsexist world, women will have an equal opportunity as men to be rejected, embarrassed, and humiliated beyond consolation.

The First Date

Boy meets girl;
girl gets boy into pickle;
boy gets pickle into girl.

—Jack Woodford (1894–1971) *on plotting*

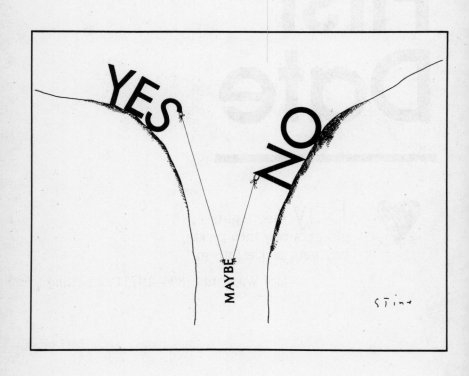

Getting Ready for a Date in Just Under Six Hours

3:55 Go on diet to lose fifteen pounds in the next five hours.

4:00 Turn on *The Oprah Winfrey Show*.

4:10 File nails.

4:20 Go to the kitchen and get a Tab.

4:30 Polish nails.

4:35 Blow on nails.

4:36 Get impatient and wave hands in air. Knock over Tab.

4:37 Curse.

4:38 Go to kitchen. Tear off paper towel carefully, using teeth.

4:45 Repolish nails on left hand. Try to be patient.

5:00 Run bath.

5:05 Call best friend and report how excited you are.

5:35 Answer doorbell. Be nice to irate downstairs neighbor. Tell him, "It's only water, for goodness sake!" Remind him that ceilings are replaceable, people are not.

5:36 Shut off running bath water.

5:37 Get into tub.

5:38 Get out of tub to answer phone.

5:39 Scream at the person who's dialed a wrong number.

5:40 Get back in tub.

5:41 Get out of tub to get another Tab.

5:43 Get in tub.

5:44 Get out of tub to get Clinique Scrub Cream.

5:45 Get in tub and fall asleep from exhaustion.

6:00 Dream about date. Remind yourself you only have three more hours left to get ready. Snap awake.

6:15 Wash hair, shave armpits and legs.

6:25 Towel dry and comb hair.

6:30 Call second-best friend. Discuss what you should wear. Ask if you can borrow her new Ralph Lauren dress. Hang up when she weasels out of the request with the lame excuse that she's wearing that dress tonight. Decide you need an alternative second-best friend.

6:45 Realize your hair is drying with funny ridges. Panic.

6:46 Run to bathroom.

6:46 Blow dry hair.

6:50 Ditto.

7:00 Ditto.

7:01 Look in mirror. Want to puke. Curse parents' hair genes.

7:02 Plug in hot rollers.

7:03 Inspect face in mirror. Decide *not* to squeeze blackheads.

7:05 Set hair with hot rollers.

7:20 Squeeze blackheads.

7:30 Get mad at yourself for squeezing blackheads. Rush to makeup case. Try to Erase red welts on your chin and forehead. Try to Erase dark circles under your eyes. Try to Erase entire face.

7:45 Get another Tab. Tweeze eyebrows, hair on chin. Wonder why hair grows so quickly on every part of your body *except* your bangs.

7:46 Prepare home for that "I just got in" look. (See section on "Date Decorating," pg. 69).

8:00 Remove hot rollers and realize you left them in too long.

8:08 Wet hair to remove some of the curl.

8:10 Use curling iron to put back some of the curl.

8:20 Apply makeup.

8:40 Rip panty hose.

8:42 Try on turtleneck sweater, making sure to smudge mascara.

8:44 Reapply eye makeup.

8:50 Decide to wear slacks.

8:52 Speed-dress—try on every outfit in the closet. Pile discards on floor.

9:01 Apply seven layers of lipstick until your lips look like you're not wearing any lipstick.

9:05 Apply a quart of mousse to your hair for that natural look.

9:14 Test breath by breathing on hand.

9:15 Answer phone.

9:16 Listen to date.

9:20 Say, "No, no problem. Maybe we can do it another time."

Getting Ready for a Date in Just Over Six Minutes

A maneuver of such precision takes split-second timing and careful preparation. The night before this operation is set to take place, assemble all the required ingredients including perfume, deodorant, Binaca, blush-on, lip gloss, hairbrush, bourbon. Before you leave for work in the morning, align ingredients around bathroom sink, being careful to place things in the above order.

7:30 Arrive home and toss everything—coat, briefcase, mail, keys, umbrella, heels—on couch. Race to bathroom.

7:31 Spray perfume.

7:31:30 Roll on deodorant.

7:32 Spritz Binaca.

7:32:30 Wipe black crud from inside eyes and under bottom lid.

7:33 Apply blush to cheeks.

7:33:30 Apply gloss to lips.

7:34 Panic when doorbell rings.

7:34:30 Sweep brush through hair.

7:35 Check teeth for lunch leftovers.

7:35:30 Belt back bourbon.

7:36 Test breath by breathing on hand. Plaster smile on
    face.
7:36:30 Open door.

Date Decorating: Preparing Your Home for His Arrival

For your first date with that special man, it is important to
create the right impression. In other words, you want to
present an image that will impress him, whether or not that
image actually projects the real you. This may be a difficult
concept for some women, especially those of us who came of
age in the late 1960s, early 1970s.

During that time we were under the misconception that we
should "let it all hang out." We told ourselves looks didn't
count, we were all beautiful human beings, what was on the
inside was much more important than what was on the outside. In hindsight, it's easy to recognize our mistake: We
failed to take into account these principles only applied if you
were under twenty-three and stoned eighteen hours a day.

Now that we know better, we need to update our standards
to be more in keeping with modern times. This is why you
must forget all that Be-Yourself, Take-Me-As-I-Am psychobabble

from your long-gone past. You are living in the material world. In the eighties, you are what you mortgage.

During these competitive times, it is perfectly permissible to use any deceit necessary to snag yourself a good date.

Your living space says a lot about who you are and how you see yourself. Consequently, it is vital that your home project an image he will admire. This is no time to split hairs, if he thinks you're rich, he may find you even more attractive.

Projecting a rich and successful image may take a lot of effort and time, depending on your bank account and on how much of a slob you really are. (This is something only you can honestly judge.) In all probability, however, you will have to spend at least as much time getting your apartment together as you would yourself.

You want to really make this guy envious of your space, so here are a few of the steps you will need to take.

First, hide all evidence that you are frivolous, superficial, or just plain stupid. Remove from view: *TV Guide*, all your confession/decorating magazines, astrology books, and/or comic books.

Store all stuffed animals in the laundry hamper. (If this is too painful, send your furry friends on an overnight sleepover with an understanding neighbor. While you're at it, deposit cat(s) and all their toys with the same neighbor. Remove all traces of kitty litter from sight and scent.)

Get rid of anything wicker, straw, or gingham. Hummels have to go. Knickknacks are definitely not eighties.

Hide all record albums or tapes by John Denver, the Boston Pops, or whales.

Stock your refrigerator with cold cuts (late night snack), lots of liquids, and breakfast (just in case).

Get out candles (but none that are carved into cute little animals or mushrooms). Stemmed candles that fit into candle holders only!

Buy yourself fresh flowers. If he asks who sent the flowers, be demure and smile. Then lie through your teeth. Say: "Just an old friend." Sigh deeply.

Hide Tampax and all other yucky personal hygiene items. You want him to think that, inside and out, you are put together as cleanly as a Barbie doll.

Try to be neat. Pick up all your dirty laundry and hide it under your bed. Stack dirty dishes in the oven or under the sink. For the sake of the female population (and his mother), you always want to maintain the illusion single women are not as messy as single men.

Overall, your apartment should be clean but not sterile. Unlike your mother, your date will not look under your couch for dustbunnies. (If he does, he should be dating your mother, not you.)

Strategically placed bits of clutter—an opened letter here, an assortment of Playbills there—tells him you are orderly but not fanatic and, more important, that your life is interesting.

If you are doing well financially, don't keep it to yourself. Display your latest tax return on the coffee table.

A computer report that you lifted from the office tells him you're involved with your job. (If he asks about the printout, reply that you don't feel like "talking shop" tonight.)

Remember that first impressions are important. To insure that he'll like you, don't be yourself. Be Susan Anton.

The First Date

Congratulations!
You've completed the two hardest tasks in the dating process:

1. You've found yourself a date.
2. You've found yourself something to wear.

You are about to embark on your first date, and you have plenty of reason to be excited. This is such a special time for you. The first date represents a wonderful moment in the dating process. This is when you and your date will develop your initial misconceptions about each other. Later on, if the relationship develops into something relatively permanent, you can look back to this time and cherish these first and lasting delusions.

But now is not the time to think about the future. You are about to face your next hurdle, and it's a big one. You must get through the first date in order to get onto the second date.

The first date is fraught with problems. Where will you go? How will you act? What will you talk about?

But let's cut to the chase here and discuss your biggest problem first.

Sex on the First Date

Should you have sex with him on the first date? If you have to ask (i.e., if that's not the sole reason for the date), then the answer is absolutely, unequivocably NO.

Researchers have calculated that the number of total dates you will have with a newfound man is directly proportionate to how many dates you wait until you have sex with him.

Sleep with a guy five minutes after you've met and your relationship will probably last as long as it takes him to lace up his Nikes.

Put the guy off until he's taken you to three movies, two plays, four museums, and three luncheons, and he's yours forever or until he decides to sleep with his secretary, his ex-wife, his ex-wife's sister, or a hairdresser named Enrique.

You must accept this: It is a proven fact that having sex on the first date is a mistake, *always*. Having sex on the first date practically guarantees that you'll never see the guy again for the following reasons:

a) If the sex is great—passionate, ecstatic, satisfying, no rope burns—he will immediately forget your last name, your telephone number, and everything else about you. It is unlikely that you will ever hear from him again.

b) If the sex is bad, you will not know each other well enough to get past the awkwardness in order to joke about the situation. He will be too embarrassed to call you again. Therefore, you will never get to the second date.

So, you see, you really cannot win.

Actually, none of this is new information. Since you were old enough to tell the difference between little girls and little boys, your mother has told you that it is always best to put a little mystery into a relationship, to hold off, and to realize that he won't buy the cow if there's always low-fat milk in the fridge. Well, the real shock is to discover that Mom was actually right about something.

So, to reiterate once more:

RULE NUMBER 1: Do not have sex with him on your first date.

RULE NUMBER 2: After you've had sex with him on the first date, don't come crying to me (or your mother) when he doesn't call you again.

RULE NUMBER 3: Don't feel guilty for being human, you little tramp.

Where to Go

Most couples prefer to go to the movies on a first date. This is a good way to spend time with another person and not have to make conversation.

You must be careful, however, in selecting a movie for the evening. You can tell a lot about a person from the kind of movies they like to see. Make sure you make the right impression. Here are some simple guidelines:

a) Avoid any recent movie written by Neil Simon or produced (and starring) Goldie Hawn. You don't want to bore each other to death on your first date.

b) Avoid movies that were hailed in the reviews as misunderstood classics. I used to be a real sucker for reviews that began, "This is one of those rare films . . ." I've seen more of these movies than I care to admit, and, invariably, it's a mistake. Don't be fooled by precious quotes or precious reviewers. Almost anything with sub-titles is also not great for a first date. You want your date to look at you during the course of the evening and not have to concentrate so hard on the screen.

c) Avoid movies that are terrible, boring, and stupid, mean-ing any movie where cars, nerds, Rob Lowe, or Burt Reynolds is given top billing.

d) Avoid, even more, movies that are terrible, boring, stupid, and violent, particularly such gems as *Death Wish, Death Wish II, Death Wish III, Missing in Action* and *Missing in Action II*. (Of course, you probably al-ready know never to see a movie starring Charles Bronson or Chuck Norris.)

e) Avoid movies that make you squirm in your seat. A General Rule of Thumb is to stay away from movies with any of the following words in their titles: HOT, HELL, INCHES, KINKY, NASTY, PEEP, SKIN, or WORKOUT.

f) A Tip About Romance Movies: According to Dr. Joyce Brothers, it is better to go see a horror movie on a date than a romantic flick. The doctor says that romance mov-ies are poor choices on a first date because they give your companion a comparison against which you'll never be able to compete. I guess the idea is that the uglier the actors on the big screen, the better your date will look to you here on earth. Therefore, don't go see Mel Gibson or Molly Ringwald in anything. If you're feeling real insecure, try a Muppets movie.

What to Eat

Never stay on your diet. Eat hearty. Don't pick at your food, and remember food is not to be played with. Do not burp loudly or otherwise embarrass your date.

What Drugs to Take

Haven't you heard that drugs are out? Drinking is out. Smoking is out. Coffee is out. Sex is out.

What's in? Money is in. Real estate is in. Investment banking is in.

About all that you can do with your date is to attend an Al-Anon meeting and, afterward, drink Perrier and discuss which mutual funds you have in common.

What to Do

Here is a good game to play during the course of your first date. This game is the fastest way I know to slyly psychoanalyze a stranger, or as they used to say in simpler times, to get to know your date.

To play this game, you ask your date four seemingly innocent questions. Write down his answers. From these answers you will be able to glean a whole mass of subconscious, probably totally bizarre, fetishes belonging to your date.

Before you get to feeling too critical, however, it might be interesting for you to first answer these questions yourself and see what's barbecuing in your own subconscious backyard.

Be sure not to peak at the answers (i.e., the hidden meanings behind the questions) before you respond to the questions, or you'll ruin the game.

Remember (and remind your date), there are no "correct" answers to these questions. Try to respond as honestly as possible without thinking too much about how your answer will be interpreted.

Here are the four questions:

1. What is your favorite animal? Describe it in three adjectives.
2. What is your favorite color? Describe it in three adjectives.
3. What is your favorite body of water? (i.e., ocean, lake, stream) Describe it in three adjectives.
4. You are in an empty white room with no openings, doors, windows, or furniture. Describe how this makes you feel in three adjectives.

HIDDEN MEANINGS:

1. His favorite animal indicates how he feels about himself. If he thinks of himself as a cute, cuddly, exotic koala bear, he's probably a nice guy to be with on Sunday morning. If his favorite animal is a slimy, poisonous killer snake, your immediate reaction might be: "Is there a back exit out of here?"
2. His favorite color denotes the way he thinks others view him. If he describes his favorite color as warm, pleasing to the eye, and "great on a sofa," you'll know he isn't threatened by you. Take your notice if he describes his favorite color as penetrating and piercing.
3. His favorite body of water is the most important category, because this is how he views sex. My last boyfriend selected the ocean and described it as eternal, foamy, and "smells good," which is as perfect a description of sex as I've ever come across. You might, however, want to be wary of the guy who chooses a river because it's treacherous and "it moves."
4. Finally, the white room is symbolic of your date's feeling about death, and here we get into the really heavy psychological stuff. Claustrophobic, frightening, and crazy are not uncommon answers. Frankly, I've never heard an answer to this question that didn't seem totally ap-

propriate except for a date who responded, "like the inside of a refrigerator" and "how much is the rent?"

What to Talk About

After you've seen a movie, finished eating dinner, and played the above game, you will probably have to engage in some kind of conversation with your date. As we all know, this can be a terrifying prospect, especially if you've taken my advice and not gotten yourself stoned beyond comprehension. Hopefully, the following guidelines may help you through the dreaded talking stage of your first date:

- If you talk about yourself, he'll think you're boring. If you talk about others, he'll think you're a gossip. If you talk about him, he'll think you are a brilliant conversationalist.

- Do not discuss bondage during the course of your conversation.

- Never whine on the first date.

- Try not to spend the entire evening asking yourself: Can I do better?

After the First Date: Debriefing Guidelines

In government, all major missions of intrigue or danger are followed by a formal debriefing procedure. Astronauts, for example, are debriefed by NASA following their flights to the moon. The CIA and the Foreign Service insist upon debriefing hostages after their ordeal with their captors.

The debriefing procedure has relevance to the dating process because, as psychologists have noted, there are many similarities between the hostage situation and the first date. Specifically, both situations involve the unwilling participation of one of the parties involved and, usually, the sex isn't so great.

Consequently, after the first date, many therapists now recommend a period of debriefing following the trauma of an initial encounter with a potential love object. Debriefing has proven useful to aid the single gal in clarifying the events of the evening as well as in easing her transition into being dateless again.

How to Evaluate Your First Date

After he says good night (or good morning, if you've been naughty), sit down in a chair and review the events of the previous evening. Carefully reassess everything that went on during your date. Compile your "Date Data" by selecting from one of the two following scenarios:

Scenario A

Description: You and your date had absolutely nothing in common. You did nothing, in fact, but argue the entire evening.

He obviously felt antagonized by almost everything you said. You felt threatened every time he opened his mouth.

You felt he was not open to a relationship, he felt you were opinionated and hostile.

You were both convinced that the other person was hung up on a past relationship.

Conclusion: You can't wait to see him again.

Estimated Time for Him to Call for Another Date: Anywhere from one week to when hell freezes over.

Recommended Course of Action: Prepare yourself to sit around and wait for the phone to ring. Stock freezer with Häagen-Dazs and lots of frozen pizzas.

Supplemental Advice: Things to do while waiting for the phone to ring: knit; learn to tap dance; date someone else.

Scenario B

Description: You and your date got along well. You agreed about most things.

He listened to your opinions and gave careful consideration to what you said. He was attentive to your needs and eager to please you.

He stayed away from topics that made you uncomfortable or on which you obviously disagreed.

At the end of the evening, he asked if he could kiss you good night. Then he asked when (and if) he could call you for another date.

Conclusion: You never want to see him again.

Estimated Time for Him to Call for Another Date: Anywhere from one hour to two hours.

Recommended Course of Action: Keep calm. Try not to think less of him because he seems to really like you. If he calls to say how much he enjoyed himself on your date, do not get nervous and tell him to drop dead.

Keep in mind this important fact: His liking you a whole lot does not necessarily mean he is a moron.

In all probability, you will not want to date this guy again; you will, in fact, not want to live in the same city as him. If, however, you have not dated in a long, long time, you may want to reconsider your initial reaction. Remember it is possible that he can change. There's always the outside chance that he was only pretending to be a sweet, considerate guy. (Some guys are incredibly adept at faking sincerity and are known in psychiatric circles as the "Donahue Impersonators.")

There's the remote possibility that, on your second date, he may completely drop his niceness facade and start seriously being mean to you.

So, try to give the guy a break. Under his sensitive veneer may lurk the heart of a bastard; perhaps he'll even turn out to be the bastard of your dreams. Think what you'll be missing if you don't give him the opportunity to show his true self. After all, every guy deserves a fair chance to treat you like dirt.

Post Debriefing

Once you are fully debriefed and have considered all your options in the wonderful world of dating, you may want to consider whether or not you wish to ever socialize again.

An Alternative to the First Date

If you decide never to go out on another date, there is an alternative activity. You can easily simulate the feelings you have when you are with a date for the first time. You can do this without having to actually date anyone. The following situations will perfectly replicate the emotional experience of a first date.

GUYS: Sit on a hot radiator and tear up ten-dollar bills.

GALS: Stand naked on a busy street corner and pretend you're not embarrassed.

First dates are so much fun!

Now, are you ready for a relationship?

Sex

 I have an intense desire to return to the womb. Anybody's.

—*Woody Allen*

What Women Want in Bed: The Width Report

In 1976, a sexologist and statistician named Sheer Height shocked the nation by publishing a book on female sexuality that she modestly called *The Height Report*. The book reported the findings of a nationwide survey where women described their most intimate feelings about sex. *The Height Report* was hailed ". . . as the best sex study since Masters and Johnson" (*The National Viewer*) and because, for many readers, ". . . it made us salivate!" (*The Beaver Observer*).

Obviously, Ms. Height's book captured the pulse of the female libido during the 1970s. However, today's sexologists note that much has changed in the field of female sexuality since Ms. Height published her landmark book. For the past decade, women have been asking: Whatever happened to the sexual revolution? Why wasn't I invited?

Major events have altered the course of sexual patterns among singles. It's surely one of the strange phenomena of this decade that the most thoughtful gift you can bring a date is not flowers, chocolates, or ankle-length pearls, but a note from your doctor.

In order to chronicle these and other changes in women's sexual habits over the past ten years, the publisher of this book financed a follow-up survey to *The Height Report*.

Sparing no expense, the publisher engaged the services of Dr. Claymore Width, Ph.D., from the McMasters Institute of Sexual Fantasies, an expert on female sexuality who was recently honored by *Ms.* magazine for his work in documenting female fantasies during intercourse. "Boy, you gals have dirty minds!" concluded the doctor.

After several months of research and development, Dr. Width finally completed a list of questions.

Just reading this questionnaire makes most women blush, all over. In fact, the questions were so personal and intimate that Dr. Width's wife immediately sued for divorce, and his mistress, Muffy, left him. Even his dog, Buffy, ran away from home.[1]

The results of this survey will shock and disarm you. We discovered many discrepancies between our findings and those of Sheer Height. Naturally, we feel our report is far superior. At the McMasters Institute, where this report was painstakingly compiled, we remind ourselves: It's not the Height that counts, it's the Width!

Findings from The Width Report

We questioned women in four basic areas of sexuality: masturbation, orgasm, sexual partners, and sexual acts.

The Height Report was probably one of the first books to openly discuss masturbation, and many people were shocked

---

[1] Editor's note: The author confuses the names here. The mistress was named Buffy and the doctor's dog was named Muffy.

to even read that word in print. Remember, though, this was before Dr. Ruth, when masturbation was still considered a subject most women didn't discuss with their parking lot attendant.

Contrary to *The Height Report*, we discovered that women were not as active in this area as Ms. Height implied in her book. On the subject of masturbation, women openly and freely gave us their honest answers. Responding to Dr. Width's question: *When you're all alone and feeling sexy, you would never, never, ever, do that nasty, disgusting, perverted thing to yourself, now would you?* Women reported:

"No! Never!"

"Of course not and how dare you ask that?"

"What do I look like, a psychopath?"

"No, Mommy, I swear, cross my heart."

Having dispelled that myth, Dr. Width went on to question women about orgasm, which professionals refer to as the Big O.

Sexologists like Dr. Width have known for years that the ways in which women experience orgasms are varied. Dr. Width asked: *How do you know when you achieve orgasm?*

He asked women to describe, in detail, what it felt like when they achieved orgasm during sex (in the missionary position and only for the purposes of procreation, of course). The responses turned out to be as varied as the women themselves.

"I go gushy all over and then I break out in hives."

"My body tenses completely and I levitate toward Mecca."

"I go completely motionless. I almost stop breathing. Once my husband gave me artificial respiration because he thought I'd died."

"I scream 'Praise the Lord' and then start singing *The Chipmunk Song*."

"I get a nosebleed."

"I vibrate, moan, have seizures, scream, claw, pant, have contractions, shudder, shiver, lose control of my pelvis, grab my partner's buttocks—and that's only for the first orgasm. By the tenth or eleventh, I really go crazy!"

"What's an orgasm?"

As much as women obviously enjoy orgasm, *The Width Report* reveals an important new element in understanding how women feel about sex. In the 1960s and 1970s, sexual discussions almost always centered around the Big O. It seemed that the single most important component of sex, for women, was orgasm. However, in this new survey, Dr. Width discovered that female sexuality today is not just a matter of achieving orgasm. The Eighties Woman wants more, much more! Here, then, is what women really want, Dr. Freud:

"It's not just orgasm I'm interested in. I also want a toaster oven."

". . . a Dustbuster."

"My boyfriend makes wild, passionate love to me and then rolls over and goes to sleep. This makes me crazy. After sex, I want him to give me a Toni home perm."

". . . tweeze my eyebrows."

"Why can't men be more considerate? I'd like my lover to think about my feelings and my needs. Just once, after he comes, he could stay awake long enough to help me polish the silverware."

The Width Report attempted to determine women's preferences in their choice of sex partners. Unfortunately, however, we could not get a scientifically accurate reading in response to our question on this subject because, for some unknown reason, Dr. Width's question about sex partners confused most of the women who responded to the questionnaire. Perhaps the question was not written clearly enough, although no one at McMasters had any trouble understanding the doctor's intention when he asked:

With whom would you prefer to have sex?
  a) Michael J. Fox
  b) Sylvester Stallone
  c) Your washing machine
  d) Fresh produce

Instead of answering this multiple-choice question, many women responded with questions of their own. They asked the doctor to clarify certain points:
"Who's Michael J. Fox?"
"Rocky I, II, III, or IV?"
"Which cycle—rinse or spin dry?"
"Steamed or raw?"
Overall, however, those who understood the question voted overwhelmingly for the fresh produce, especially if it came with guacamole dip.
Dr. Width's next multiple-choice question asked women to select their favorite sexual act. Due to certain copyright laws and the publisher's definition of what constitutes pornography, we are not allowed to reprint the specific choices of sexual acts that Dr. Width offered in this question.[2] However, the results of this question, in terms of which sex *act* women prefer, confirmed that the majority of women preferred answer (d): intercourse with a human being.
These responses constitute the major findings of *The Width Report*.[3] In all, the questionnaire was mailed to over four

----

[2]Note to the public: This question was specifically cited in Dr. Width's divorce hearing, and, after it was read aloud in open court, Mrs. Width was awarded custody of the children, the house, the record collection, and everything Dr. Width had ever touched without rubber gloves.

[3]For readers who are interested, a more detailed assessment is available through the McMasters Institute for an unbelievably exorbitant fee, proof that you are over twenty-one, and a promise to perform a sex act of your choice with Dr. Width.

million women. We received answers from thirteen women from all different parts of the country.

We wondered why so many of these women took the time and effort to read through this gargantuan questionnaire, so we called each and every one and asked why they'd responded. Their answers varied:

"It's time women spoke out about sex!"

"I was under the dryer with nothing else to do."

"I was too young to get in on *The Height Report*, so I'm real glad I had another opportunity."

"Answering this questionnaire got me hot!"

"My husband made me do it while he watched."

There are many conclusions that can be drawn from the result of *The Width Report*, not the least of which is whether Dr. Width should be allowed to practice in the continental United States. But the overall response to this questionnaire has led Dr. Width and his colleagues at the McMasters Institute to conclude that women today feel that, in the best of all possible worlds, sex would be something they could enjoy without always getting asked to answer questionnaires all the time.

"Wouldn't it be great if we just did it, instead of getting tested all the time?" wrote one housewife from Des Moines. "I get six or seven questionnaires a week, there's hardly enough room in my mailbox for my Publisher's Clearing House correspondence with Ed McMahon. What I want to know is: When am I going to actually get paid for all this information? Sheer Height made a bundle on her book, but did I see a single dime for all my work? No. It ain't fair. Talk about getting screwed!"

Take This Test: Am I a Good Lover, or What?

Are you a good lover, or what?

This is a question that can only partially be answered by you alone. Your Significant Other probably has a pretty knowledgeable opinion on the subject, so you should take this test together.

Score five points every time you and your Significant Other agree on an answer.

If you don't have a lover, take the test twice and see how well you get along with yourself.

1. The most important factor in a relationship is:

   a) mutual respect
   b) compatible astrology signs

2. My favorite fragrance is:

   a) Calvin Klein's Obsession
   b) Windex

3. If your date suggested using a condom during intercourse, would you ask:

   a) "What's a condom?"
   b) "What's intercourse?"

4. When your lover does something during sex that turns you off, do you:

   a) pretend to enjoy it to spare his feelings
   b) scream, "STOP THAT!!!"

5. Do you use sex as:

   a) a reward
   b) a punishment

6. Does your current Significant Other enjoy sex:

   a) with the lights on
   b) with someone else

7. Your preferred method of birth control is:

   a) to use a diaphragm
   b) to mention marriage

8. The idea of oral sex makes you:

   a) salivate
   b) regurgitate

9. An unmade bed describes:

   a) your favorite playing field
   b) the way he looks in clothes

10. The last person who sent you flowers was:

    a) your Significant Other
    b) the dinner guest who got sick all over your bathroom floor

11. Sex with a total stranger is:

    a) immoral
    b) your definition of marriage

12. Who wrote the book of love?

    a) Alex Comfort
    b) your accountant

13. When your lover doesn't get aroused, you:

    a) say, "That's okay, honey."
    b) pick up the phone and call someone else

14. You believe love:

    a) makes the world go round
    b) is as good an excuse as any

15. Your sex life is:

    a) your business
    b) everybody's business

16. During sex you think about:

    a) your lover
    b) your doorman

17. For a romantic date, you'd serve a bottle of:

    a) French champagne
    b) Gatorade

18. Home is where:

    a) your heart is
    b) you keep your VCR

19. You don't need a lot of money because:

    a) you have your health
    b) you have your credit cards

20. You like having money because:

    a) you can help others
    b) you're hard on shoes

21. Your most erotic zone is:

    a) your neck
    b) tow-away

22. You need sex:

   a) every day
   b) every leap year

23. You are really impressed if your lover:

   a) goes out of his way to please you
   b) wants to know your last name

OPTIONAL QUESTIONS:

24. Why are you taking this test?

   a) It's here
   b) You hope to improve yourself

25. If a test told you to jump out of the window would you do it?

   a) No
   b) Only if it would make your breasts firmer

SCORING:

75–125: You and your lover are really compatible. You see eye to eye on almost everything. You have a lot in common and are perfectly suited for each other. I give your relationship one week.

45–74: You and your lover share the basic ingredients necessary for a satisfying sexual relationship. You agree on some of the most important things and are therefore relatively compatible. If one of you has a lot of money, your relationship has potential.

0–44: Obviously, you two have absolutely nothing in common, which means you are incredibly hot together. Be forewarned that you are in serious danger of a fatal attraction that may result in a long-term commitment. Proceed with extreme caution.

Optional Questions: If you answered either of these questions, deduct fifty points from your test score. Go to the nurse's office and get a pass to go home. You are suffering severe test stress. You need to cut down immediately. You are absolutely forbidden to read *Cosmo* for the next six months.

Relation-
ships

 What goes up must come down. But don't expect it to come down where you can find it.

—Jane Wagner
The Search for Signs of Intelligent Life in the Universe

Relation-
ships

What Is a Healthy Relationship?

What constitutes a healthy relationship between a man and a woman? This question has plagued singles since the invention of the Sock Hop.

The concept of a healthy relationship was first described in 1983 by the German psychiatrist Dr. Zigfried Frung in his landmark paper, *What Makes Dick and Jane Run Together?*

"In the healthy relationship," claimed Dr. Frung, "you will not spend more than fifteen minutes per evening worrying that your friends will think less of you when they meet your date."

Previous to the publication of Dr. Frung's paper, it was generally accepted that a healthy couple didn't fight all the time. "This is simply not true," stated Dr. Frung. "A healthy couple fights about every insignificant detail and then has great sex. In an unhealthy relationship, the couple fights about every insignificant detail *during* sex."

In writing about sex, Dr. Frung makes frequent reference to the work of Masters and Johnson and Johnson, a team of psychiatrists who gained fame in the late 1960s for their work with ménage à trois relationships.

"In a healthy relationship between only two people," wrote Masters and Johnson and Johnson, "you do not wake up in the mornings wondering: How quickly can I get this person out of my apartment?

"This rule of thumb is, however, mitigated if, before you've brushed your teeth or had a cup of coffee, your date says, '*I think I'm insulted by what you said last night*' and expects you to care."

According to Dr. Frung's observations, sexual compatibility in a healthy relationship is strengthened if both partners realize that compromise is essential. The real paradox for today's singles is that they spend the greater part of their adult life refining and improving themselves to the point of perfection and then have to compromise to keep their love object (who was the reason they wanted to be perfect in the first place). "People who would love to take the *settle* out of settle down," said Masters, "but it don't work that way."

Many of Frung's early observations have survived virtually intact and are as fresh as this morning's newspaper headlines. For example, a major theme of Dr. Frung's work is the concept of Dating Down. "In a healthy relationship, the man dates up the social ladder and the woman dates down. This changes radically for men after marriage. Married men always date down after their wedding vows. Married women, however, continue in their previous pattern by dating their pool boys and car mechanics."

The proof of Dr. Frung's observation was recently verified by Gary Hart, who is a textbook example of someone who married up (his wife was the daughter of a college president) and yet dated down (his girlfriend was an actress-slash-model).

Dr. Frung maintains that the American public was first exposed to a healthy relationship on the early television show, *That Girl!*, which starred Marlo Thomas as a perky actress-slash-model who dated her next-door neighbor, Don. Unfortunately, the show was cancelled due to its high boredom factor, which is, coincidentally, also the reason why most healthy relationships are terminated.

Dr. Frung's theories on the existence of a healthy relationship have not gone uncontested. A conflicting body of opinion maintains there is no such thing as a healthy relationship. Dr. Juend, one of the major opponents of the healthy relationship concept, argues, "Most couples aren't really in love, they just act that way to aggravate their single friends."

Apparently, most singles in today's dating pool question the very existence of the so-called healthy relationship.

In a recent Harrison poll, when asked for a definition of a healthy relationship, most singles replied, "Duh?"

In fact, many people cannot psychologically accept the rigors of such arrangements. "I've tried healthy relationships," claims thirty-seven-year-old bachelor Hawk Zipkin, "but, I don't know, I feel more comfortable in a neurotic situation. I think severe psychological humiliation and daily traumatic assaults on my masculinity makes life more interesting. Don't you?"

In an article for *Cosmo*, Dr. Frung advised readers about the two specific feelings that signal the onset of an unhealthy relationship.

1. The feeling that you've lowered your standards beyond a "reasonable" amount.
2. After your first evening together, the only definitive conclusion you've reached is that you would've had a better time alone, even in bed.

Getting through the "Firsts" without suffering a massive anxiety attack is one of Dr. Frung's main criteria for forming a healthy relationship. For example, after spending your first night together, you should not consider it an unfair obligation to make your date a cup of coffee in the morning. The other important such Firsts, as noted by Dr. Frung, include: the First Shower Together, First Full Weekend, First Party with His Friends, First Dinner with Your Friends, First Time You Cook for Him, and your First Pregnancy Scare.

In the *Grimness Book of World Records*, the world's longest running healthy relationship began in 1970 when Tom Bitterman, a high school freshman from Terre Haute, Indiana, asked out Florence Barclay, a Born Again cheerleader, also of Terre Haute. The two became instantly inseparable. Within a week, they'd invented pet names for each other.

The Tom and Florence Phenomenon, as it was later called in psychiatric circles, was, according to Dr. Frung, "so normal that it was disgusting."

Tom and Florence used baby talk to communicate with each other, often inflicting this revolting language on their friends.

The couple constantly referred to themselves as "we," although, when separated, Tom mentioned Florence's name twenty-six times a day and Florence averaged a whopping thirty-three times.

They began to dress alike, favoring plaid flannel shirts and matching scarves. On campus they were known as Ken and Barbie.

Tom claimed to love Florence's mother.

The couple scored 99 percent on every *Cosmo* compatibility test they ever took together.

In restaurants, Tom ordered Florence's meals; she cut his meat.

Tom bought Florence so much candy that, in one college semester, she gained twenty-five pounds, as did her dorm mother.

The couple waited approximately eight years, until they were married, to have sex.

At their tenth high school reunion, Tom Bitterman announced that his marriage ". . . was still a bowl of cherries.

We were never happier. No man alive could ask for a better wife than my little Florie-Dorie."

"Oh, Flubby-Dub," cooed Florence.

Enraged, the crowd of fellow classmates (who were mostly divorced and/or desperately single) jeered the Bittermans off the dance floor. Two months later, alumni from the Class of 1974 voted unanimously to blackball Tom and Florence from all future high school reunions. Their names were permanently stricken from the yearbook. Tragically, they were retroactively impeached as king and queen of the senior prom.

Neighbors in Terre Haute began to shun the ever-smiling couple. The Bitterman home was bombarbed with phony phone calls, nasty letters, and rotten eggs. One night, a group of neighbors, dressed in white sheets, defaced the Bitterman home with the four cruelest words in the English language. Across the two-car garage, the angry crowd painted the slogan, "Have a Nice Day!" A week later, the mob returned and fire-burned a smiling Happy Face on the Bittermans' front lawn.

After the Bittermans' appeal for state protection was denied by the governor (who was, coincidentally, a college acquaintance of Tom's and a bitter, twice-divorced father of six), they were forced to sell their house and move to another state. Under a federal protection program, the Bittermans are now living under an assumed name, posing as an unhappily married couple.

What Dr. Frung failed to acknowledge in his paper was that the healthy relationship can pose a serious threat of jealous rage, provoking otherwise peace-loving friends and neighbors to acts of violence; certainly, one of the main reasons why healthy relationships are so rare in today's society.

Dear Dating Maven: Answers to Reader Mail

Dear Dating Maven,

I have a problem with my boyfriend, Jeff. He's always talking about how much he hates himself. He says that if I break up with him, he'll really go berserk. Sometimes he talks about killing himself. In fact, I spent most of our last date talking him in off the window ledge.

His behavior has taken the romance out of the relationship, and I'm thinking about not seeing him anymore. But then I wonder: Should I take all this suicide stuff seriously?

Also, if I dump Jeff, will I be able to find another date for my sister's wedding?

Cora

Dear Cora,

It's difficult to fully analyze your situation considering you did not provide me with a great deal of information. In order to properly advise you, I need answers to the following questions: How much does Jeff earn a year? Is he husband material? And, what are your chances of attracting a new guy? What is the condition of your inner thighs?

Suicide is serious business and needs careful deliberation. Without understanding all the ramifications I cannot tell you or Jeff what to do.

Dating M.

Dear Dating M,

Jeff is an unemployed mime performer with a serious drinking problem. Also, he likes to dress up like a French maid and dust my bookshelves.

I am a sales rep for a major pharmaceutical company and I support both of us.

I jog ten to twenty miles a day. My inner thighs have been compared to aluminum siding.

Cora

Dear Cora,

Open your windows and wear a miniskirt to the office.

DM

Dear DM,

All through Jeff's funeral, I kept wondering: Why do my relationships always end badly? I really do want to get seriously involved with a man. What am I doing wrong?

I was nuts about my boyfriend before Jeff. His name was Tony and he was such a great guy that

I didn't even mind when he'd ask me to scoop up after his Great Dane.

When Tony left me for his brother's ex-second-wife, I stayed in bed for ten days and cried myself a river.

How can I avoid getting hurt like this again?

Cora from Detroit

Dear Cora,

There's a simple solution to your dating dilemma. Only date men you don't like.

Actually, the more repulsive, the better.

This way, when they dump you, you will not care.

D. Maven

Dear D. Maven,

I took your advice and now I'm dating a man I can't stomach.

Dick is a successful periodontist who insists that we floss before sex. He's an awful dresser and I really hate his hair.

Dick and I have been seeing each other for almost two months, and if he ever decides to dump me, I'll thank my lucky stars.

Dick's thirty-fifth birthday is next week and I don't know what to get him. The only gift he claims to want is an "official" *Star Trek* uniform. When I ask him why he wants such a thing he blushes and can't give me a reason.

Don't you think he's a little old for this? What am
I to make of his request?

Not A Trekkie

Dear Not A Trekkie,
What rank uniform does Dick want?

DM

Dear DM,
Science Officer.
Leonard Nimoy (Mr. Spock) is like a god to Dick.

Cora

Dear Cora,
Any rank lower than Captain is unacceptable.

Dating Maven

Dear Dating Maven,
Dick hated the electric shaver I bought him for
his birthday and we broke up a week later.
I was thrilled to have him out of my life, but I
still really want to get married. I mean, I *really* want
to get married. What can I do?

Guess Who?

Dear Cora,

Do not despair. There is a huge, untapped pool of
men who will not only marry you but who'll pay
you $1,500 for the privilege. These men are called
immigrants or aliens (but are not the kind from
Mars).

These available men need to marry a woman of
your obvious social position (i.e., American) in order to get their green cards and stay in this country.

Although these marriages are often belittled as
"marriages of convenience," single women know
that marriage to anyone is always more convenient
than being single.

To find an immigrant, you can hang out in China-
town or visit a Third World country. Good luck!

DM

Dear Dating Maven,

My new boyfriend and I saw you on Dr. Ruth's
TV show last week. Juan José thought you were
"muy bueno" and I thought you were very good, too.

I couldn't help notice the huge diamond on your
finger. I told Juan José the ring had to be a fake,
right?

Cora

Dear Cora,

The only thing that's fake about me are my tits.

DM

Dear Dating Maven,
 I travel a lot on my job so I'm separated several
nights a week from my husband. How can I tell if
Juan José is unfaithful to me?
                                Concerned in Detroit

Dear Concerned,
 If your husband is very affectionate (especially
around other people) and if he always wants to
make love, you can generally assume that he is fooling around with another woman. On the other
hand, I wouldn't complain if I were you.
                                Dating Maven

Dear Dating Maven,
 Juan José and I divorced about six months ago.
(I left him for my male secretary.) We had no chil-
dren so we don't get to see each other at all anymore.
 The problem is that I think I still love my Juan
José and I've heard that he still loves me. I would
like to build a new relationship with him but I'm
embarrassed after all the verbal abuse we flung
at each other in divorce court.
 Should I try seeing him again?
                                Ex-Señora

Dear Ex-Señora,

Dating A.D. (After Divorce), especially an ex-husband, is very difficult business and should be considered only if you haven't had any sex in a very long time, which, from the sound of your office situation, is not the case.

However, in your favor is that you are also Dating B.C. (Before Children), which does make it easier because there are no witnesses if you make a fool of yourself.

Why not call your ex and feel him out? Better yet, drop off where he works. It's always better to feel someone out in person.

                                                        DM

Dear DM,

I hardly get any sleep at all any more. Baby Maven José is up all night screaming.

What can I do about severe diaper rash?

                                                        Cora

Dear Cora,

Sorry, diaper rash is Ann Landers' domain. Kisses to Baby Maven.

                                                        DM

Dating Younger Men

Let's get personal for a minute. What are we to really think of dating a younger man?

In order to examine this ever-growing phenomenon, we interviewed Kelly Koran, an attractive strawberry blonde who hangs out at Jillsy's Bar and Grill in downtown Seattle. Kelly had a lot to tell us about the younger man/older woman scene.

In Kelly's own words:

Hi! Is the tape rolling? My name's Kelly.

I guess you could call me a modern woman of the eighties. I own a Gold American Express card and lots of sexy underwear.

Excuse me. Tom? I'll have another Dewar's on the rocks, double, okay?

Where was I? Oh, yeah, about me. I've always prided myself on my openness. People will say to me, "Kelly, I love the color of your hair. Is it natural?"

"Natural? Sure!" I reply. "For seventy-five bucks, you can have natural too!" [Laughter, quite loud]

Now, about my age I'm scrupulously honest. I'm thirty-nine and proud of it. I'm the best I can be. I've learned to like myself. I've learned to like scotch. [Laughter] No, seriously, though. I'm so much more *together* than I was in my twenties.

The way things are today, I'd never want to be a teenager again.

Hey! I'm not getting older, I'm getting richer. In fact, to quote Mister Entertainment, Henny Youngman, "I've got all the money I'll ever need, if I die by four o'clock." [Laughter]

Tom? Another round for me and the reporter, here. No? OK, just me then.

Okay, now you were asking about younger men? Listen, last week, across this very same crowded bar stool, I met a gorgeous guy. Gorgeous? I swear he was a young Michael J. Fox. Really, fabulous. And the buns on him! We get to talking, you know, kind of flirting like, and after a couple of beers, he mentions he's twenty-seven years old.

Good God, I think to myself.

"Good gracious," I say to him, "you're a baby!"

"No way," he says, "I'm not that much younger than you."

Now, my best friend, Cindy's, sitting right next to me, and Cindy says, "Yeah, that's true, Kelly's only thirty-one."

I smiled and didn't correct her.

"You see what I mean?" says this fabulous hunk. "You ain't so much older."

So I'd really done it. I'd lied about my age. Well, I kind of thought lying would help to, you know, cement things between me and Mr. Twenty-seven. [Deep sigh] It didn't.[1]

I don't really think lying about your age ever helps a relationship . . . although sometimes it makes for a really interesting one-night stand. [Laughter]

Well, you get my drift, right? So, how old are you? Yeah? That's great. Twenty-seven's great. Umm.

The French, you know, they say by the time a woman's

---

[1]For a more detailed explanation see "Sex on the First Date," page 73.

forty, she gets the face she deserves. So, what'd you think?
I got the face I deserve? No, don't answer that, I'm only
kidding. I ain't near forty yet.

Tom? One more.

[Loud gulping, ice cubes rattling]

Hell, what do the French know, anyway. Am I right? Or
what? I mean, they don't even use deodorant. How smart
can they be?

Anyway, I come to the conclusion it's probably better to
be honest about your age. Like honesty's the best policy
and all that stuff.

All the movie stars, you know, they all date younger men
and no one bats an eyelash. Like for instance, Priscilla
Presley's forty-one and she lives with a thirty-year-old guy.
She just had a baby, at forty-one, you know? I think she
married this guy, the father, but I'm not sure. I know they
were living together. And, like Sigourney Weaver, from
Aliens, she's thirty-six and her husband's like thirty. Also,
Kathleen Turner? Thirty-six, and her husband's thirty or
thirty-one.

I know what I'm talking about here because I read *People*
magazine every week.

Speaking about Kathleen Turner, I read in some article
her husband said to her, "I may not know everything in the
world about sex, but I know what you like." Isn't that just
the most romantic thing you've ever heard? [Sigh]

But the point is, all this makes me wonder, you know: Is
this a trend or what? Are there only thirty-year-old men in
Hollywood?

My friend Cindy says all the forty-year-old guys are
dating eighteen-year-olds.

Cindy should know, she dated a younger guy—and I
mean, younger—for a real long time, until the day he
found her Erno Laszlo black soap in the bathroom and said,

"My mom uses this." Poor Cindy discovered she was only five years younger than Mikey's *mother*.

Jeez, his mother!

I gotta have another drink, just thinking about that's downright depressing. Come on, Tom, set 'em up, pal, Palsy-walsy. Don't this joint have the cutest bartenders? Tommy, hey, Tommy, come here, yeah, over here. What time you off tonight? Oh. How about tomorrow?

Yeah, well, actually, I'm busy, too. I just forgot. [Laughter] I mean, I have this thing. No, really, don't worry about it. Listen, I think I'll switch to brandy, okay? Thanks. [Long exhale]

You know, I'd really, really like to have a few words with the joker who said, "You're not getting older, you're getting better."

Better? Okay bub, I'd say to him, I'll tell you what's better: my eggplant parmigiana and my relationship with my shrink.

Wanna know what's worse? My gums, my fear of catching some fatal sex disease, my skin tone, my visits to the gynecologist, my upper arms, my eyes. I can't read a blessed thing anymore without my damn glasses. And, I'm not even going to mention my thighs.

Better? Better, my ass.

Jus' make me twenty-three again, for jus' one more decade, and I'll show you better.

But, NO, we aren't allowed to turn back the clock, are we? No siree, bob. We make the teensy-weensy mistake of getting a little older and we're stuck with it forever.

The truth is: I'm Not Getting Older, I'm Getting **OLDER!!!!!**

[Weeping obscures the next couple of sentences on the tape.]

Say, ya know, you're a very nice person, so I'm gonna

tell ya something. I made a big decision. In my next life I'm coming back as Tina Turner—then it won't matter how old I get, I'll always have great legs.

'Scuse me, but I think I'm gonna be sick. Cindy, help me to the ladies', would ya?"

K elly's story teaches us many lessons. First and foremost, of course, that drinking and interviewing don't mix. Second, that lying about your age probably doesn't help a relationship.

We also see that Kelly is not particularly pleased about getting older.

What about you?

Are you currently dating a man who's too young for you?

This is difficult to determine because everyone always says, "Age is relative." Everyone over thirty, that is.

An easy test, however, can demonstrate whether or not your current lover is too young for you. Simply answer the following four questions:

1. Is his idea for a great date:

   a) movie and dinner
   b) playing video games

2. When his mother calls, does she say:

   a) "When are you coming to dinner?"
   b) "Make sure my son wears his raincoat today."

3. Is his favorite make-out music:

   a) Johnny Mathis
   b) Twisted Sister

4. Does he think Heavy Metal is:

  a) toxic

  b) easy listening music

If you answered (a) to most of these questions then you are in just the right age group. If you answered (b) then perhaps you might want to consider any of the following four procedures: plastic surgery, suction lipectomy, collagen shots, and nail wrapping.

After all, if it's good enough for Cher, why not you?

Dating Married Men

Sooner or later in the dating process, every unattached female is bound to encounter, date, and fall in love with a married man. Among single women, it is said that falling in love with a married man is as inevitable as shopping malls.

We know that women have dated married men for centuries, but it was not until the publication of *Sex and the Single Girl* that the practice of adultery was both sanctioned and encouraged.

Written with the same editorial integrity that Helen Gurley Brown would later employ when establishing *Cosmopolitan* magazine, *Sex and the Single Girl* formulated the then-scandalous thesis that (a) it was okay for single girls to sleep

with married men and (b) it was even better if the girls
enjoyed it!

Critics argued there was a basic misconception at the heart
of this book. While *Sex and the Single Girl* promised to
"explode the myth that a girl must be married to enjoy a
satisfying life," in the very first sentence of the book, Helen
Gurley Brown boasted of being married to the man of her
dreams, owning two Mercedes-Benzes, and having a full-time
maid. If the single life was so great, argued some critics, why
did Mrs. Brown feel compelled to let us know she was no
longer dateless and desperate?

"She's got no right to preach to single gals," wrote a thirty-
four-year-old single gal from Hackensack, New Jersey (from
the 3/24/64 issue of *Real Confessions* magazine). "I don't take
advice from my married sister, why should I listen to this
Gurley dame?"

Yet despite such attacks, Mrs. Brown surely struck a reso-
nant chord when she described the reasons why single gals
are more attractive to men than married ladies are. Here is
where the author reveals a genuine gift for translating complex intellectual and psychological motivations into a language
that any layperson can easily grasp. "She [the single gal] has
more time and often more money to spend on herself. She has
the extra twenty minutes to exercise every day, an hour to
make up her face for their date. She has all day Saturday to
whip up a silly, wonderful cotton brocade tea coat to entertain
him in the next day or hours to find it at a bargain sale."

As if this insight wasn't enough, the author continues to
astound the reader by providing the kind of advice that only
someone of Mrs. Brown's stature is qualified to give.

"As for cooking for married men, that's sheer insanity!"
advises Mrs. Brown. "One reason you see them is to add
glamour to your life. Once in a while you may honor a
married man with a dinner invitation, or let's put it this way:

If he comes trooping over with two mallard ducks he shot especially for you and a bottle of Cordon Bleu, cook his dinner."

Is it any wonder that *Sex and the Single Girl* was an enormous best-seller? Never before had any book explained in such detail the etiquette involved when our gentlemen callers tossed us a couple of bloody duck corpses. It was so reassuring to finally understand the proper method of handling this potentially embarrassing situation, especially since it comes up so often in the life of a single gal!

In general, the practice of dating married men has increased substantially since the days of Mrs. Brown. (We have to wonder if anyone is dating Mr. Brown and, if so, what does Mrs. Brown have to say about that?)

The reasons for the rise in dating married men is best explained by Ms. Mavis Davis, president of the *Are You a Fabulous Single Person?* dating agency of Oklahoma City, which specializes in arranging S&M (Singles and Marrieds) dates.

"There are more single gals around and not nearly enough men," says Ms. Davis, "so we have to borrow from the married pool to fill in the shortage.

"Besides, single gals, like myself, enjoy dating married men because there's a great deal of stability in the relationship," explains Ms. Davis. "You always know where you stand with a married man—directly behind the proverbial eight ball.

"The adulterous relationship has many other benefits as well. For example, it helps cement our feelings of insecurity and abandonment. At the same time, an affair with a married man reinforces what our moms always told us: No one will ever love us like our mothers. Actually, the joke is that married men love us *exactly* like our mothers in that they allow us no control over the relationship and require us to constantly tell them how great they are!"

Ms. Davis is herself currently involved in a ten-year relationship with a married man whose identity she refused to reveal. "His last name is Hucklestratmeyerhaus and his family lives in Wilbur, Oklahoma, on Jonestown Street," she said, "but that's *all* I'll tell you."

In promoting her dating agency, Ms. Davis recently published a pamphlet promoting the advantages of the S&M relationship. Entitled *Do You Enjoy Afternoon Sex?*, the book is given free of charge to all clients of the agency. In it, Ms. Davis explains the many advantages of dating a married man. For example:

You'll never have to be nice to his mother.

You'll always have a substantial excuse for your depression, lethargy, neurosis, and/or extra ten pounds.

You'll have lots of free time on the weekends and during Christmas vacation to wash your hair, see your friends, and feel rejected.

Running off to a hotel during lunch hour is a great way to stick to your diet.

You'll have a good reason to cry at movies.

You're in the glamorous company of such monumental love affairs as Tracy and Hepburn.

You don't have to deal with his dental appointments or laundry.

You don't have to pretend to be interested in his children.

You'll always miss him and he'll always be beholden to you, so the sex will usually be good, if not great.

You never have to attend funerals of his relatives or his family dinners.

You'll get plenty of practice delivering ultimatums. (See chapter on "Ultimatums and Their Relationship to Holding Grudges," page 123.)

Once you agree to date married men, you quadruple your odds of getting a date.

"All in all, it's not such a bad deal," adds Ms. Davis.

"You're relieved from many of the monotonous chores of matrimony and, very often, married men will pay your shrink bills. And, of course, you never have to worry that he'll divorce you. That beats sitting home and watching *Wheel of Fortune*, doesn't it?"

Breaking Up

 Who's Virginia?

>—Rose Kennedy, when asked why her daughter-in-law Joan lived in Boston while her son Ted lived in Virginia.

 Your life should be filled with lawyers!

>—Yiddish curse

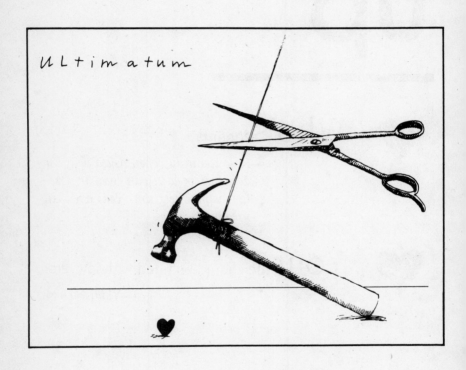

Ultimatum

Ultimatums and Their Relationship to Holding Grudges

In the logical sequence of dating events, the first date leads to sex and then turns into the dreaded state called a relationship. The length of the formal relationship period is dependent upon many factors, including ex-girlfriends, commitment phobias, and the frequency of oral sex. Nonetheless, it almost always culminates in the process known as the ultimatum.

(It is interesting to note that the word "ultimatum" comes from the Greek word *ultimatata-tum* which, literally translated, means "Do it or die, you creep.")

As is true for many traditional dating rituals, the ultimatum encounter is usually witless, degrading, and almost touchingly absurd.

Like neurosurgery, delivering the ultimatum is the most delicate of all procedures and needs to be handled very, very carefully in order to prevent permanent brain damage and irreparable ego scarring.

At the end of such an encounter, the single woman is either engaged or, most likely, hysterically dateless again.

Because there is such a great risk involved when employing the ultimatum, many women delay this stage, sometimes for months, sometimes for years, and sometimes until she can no longer remember why she wanted him in the first place.

This dilemma often motivates single women to seek psychiatric help. In fact, psychiatrists report that two most often asked questions by single women when beginning therapy are:

1. How can I get the courage to deliver an ultimatum to my boyfriend?
2. How much do you charge for a session?

The answer to the ultimatum question, as so many answers you'll receive from your therapist, is quite simply: "How do you feel about that?"

(You can calculate your therapist's fee by using the following formula: Think of the most outrageous amount of money a person could conceivably charge for listening to you talk for forty minutes. Then multiply that figure by fifteen.)

How to Deliver an Ultimatum

It is a well-documented fact that the ultimatum comes up most often in relationships between single women and married men. During these affairs, women really get an opportunity to hone their ultimatum delivery technique, which will prove very useful later in life when (and if) these women ever become mothers. (No one on earth is better at delivering an ultimatum than a mother.)

Single women dating single men can learn a lot about the fine art of delivering the ultimatum by studying the two most common procedures employed when delivering an ultimatum to a married man.

First, there is the technique known as the Ultimatum Retrieved (UR), which is when the ultimatum is delivered but not enforced. The following conversation between a married man and a single woman is an excellent example of the UR.

She: "Leave your wife, or else!"
He: "Or else, what?"
She: "Or else, I'm going out with Herb in Accounting."
He: "You couldn't do that to me." (Optional: Voice breaks)
She: "Please, don't cry."
He: "You won't go out with Herb?"
She: "No, I suppose not."
He: "Great. How about Mexican for dinner?"

The UR, in its various disguises, can continue for years and years, long after Herb has left the accounting department.

The Counter Ultimatum (CU) is a more sophisticated technique for silencing the threat of the initial ultimatum and is apparent in an exchange such as:

She: "Leave your wife or I'll kill myself."
He: "If you kill yourself, I'll kill myself."
She: "Really?"
He: "I couldn't live without you. Don't you know that, kitten?"
She: "I guess I do."
He: "Great. How about Mexican for dinner?"

In both these cases, the married man neutralizes the ultimatum and thus buys himself more time. Eventually, however, the ultimatum is delivered once too often and the relationship splits apart. This is followed by a long period of tears and recriminations.

While this is a very difficult period, it is not without its advantages. It is during this time that women can work on their capacity to develop and cultivate a grudge.

How to Hold a Grudge

Of course, we know that some people are quick to forgive; they're basically decent and kind. They don't like confrontation and they keep their temper and their complaints to themselves. They have learned the fine art of turning the other cheek. They would never try to steal your boyfriend. They do not think of suing if they slip on your doormat. They never let their answering machines pick up a call when they are home. These people are not properly adjusted to life in the eighties and should be avoided at all costs. It's only a matter of time before these people become hopelessly addicted to *The Cosby Show* and Valium.

Modern times demand appropriate action, introspection, and self-absorption. You cannot function today without the proper defense mechanisms, such as holding a grudge.

How good you are at grudge maintenance will depend on the strength of two very specific personality traits: a long memory and a short temper.

A really good memory is most important. You will need to train your brain to function like a computer; to store every hurt, every slight—sometimes for years—until the proper moment. Retrieval of this data is most appropriate during the course of a heated argument, when your adversary is most vulnerable. Then you can fling your well-aimed grievance for maximum damage.

Second, you need a short temper, which you will use both as an excuse to release your venom and as your explanation for being really mean, rotten, and selfish. (Actually, you do not need to be mean, rotten, and selfish; as long as your mother continually accuses you of these things. Eventually, you will start to believe her.)

To practice your capacity to hold a grudge against a former lover, it is wise to practice with your immediate family. In general, scientists note that it's best to save your worst grudges for relatives. This is called "keeping it in the family" and is effective because you've known your family for a long time and are apt to have a history of complaints and lots of old wounds you can bring up at the crucial moment.

Just think, if you can develop a healthy enough grudge against the majority of your relatives, you may never again have to attend another family get-together. Instead of driving two hours in traffic to spend another two hours arguing with your brother-in-law, you'll be able to spend the afternoon at home, watching a movie on your VCR and eating lots of junk food before dinner, peacefully ruining your appetite.

After parents and siblings, the best grudges are those held against spouses, especially ex-spouses, with lovers and ex-lovers running a close second. The most educational grudges are about family feuds, divorce debates, jealous friendships, and unrequited love. After a hefty fight with your mother or a nasty plate-throwing evening with your future ex-boyfriend, you will be much more prepared to face life in the office.

If you begin practicing young enough, it is possible to still be holding a grudge against your high school boyfriend while you are celebrating the birth of your first grandchild.

The great thing about holding a grudge is that you really do get better at it with age and that, unlike innocence or happiness, it's truly one of those emotions that, with a little effort, will never desert you.

The Five Stages of Dying from a Broken Heart

Can you actually die of a broken heart? Although a broken heart is only one chapter in the great Book of Love, it's an especially ugly one.

The actual process by which we recover from a broken heart has been studied in detail by Dr. Elaine Kahula-Rossi. An eminent psychotherapist specializing in obsessional behavior in San Francisco, Dr. Kahula-Rossi was on sabbatical for a year and living on a small island in the Puget Sound area near Seattle, Washington, when she accidentally became involved with several brokenhearted people.

During her early morning walkies with her dog, Friskie, the doctor came upon several brokenhearted people who'd washed ashore during the night. Some of these people had drifted up from as far away as Los Angeles and San Diego.

The sight of these depressed, sunburnt, bloated people sparked the good doctor's curiosity. She began to study the effects of rejection and salt water, and wondered whether there was a pattern to the process of recovering from getting dumped.

Almost immediately, the doctor noted that although her patients were different ages, religions, and sexual preferences, all of them seemed to display similar characteristics. She closely observed these people and spent many hours listening to them discuss their former love objects, supplementing her personal observations with extensive research from back issues of *Cosmopolitan* and *Glamour* magazine.

Ultimately, Dr. Kahula-Rossi concluded there were five stages in the process of dying from a broken heart. A few years later, however, Dr. Kahula-Rossi added on a sixth stage in order to placate her patients who demanded an even half-dozen.

Denial

The first stage is denial, where the patient refuses to acknowledge her pain. This stage is most often characterized by the twin expressions, "I never liked him anyway, so there," and "he wasn't that good in bed, not really."

The patient in denial refuses to accept reality. "I'm sure he'll call tomorrow," patients will say again and again.

It is during denial that patients are most likely to believe one of the three most common myths of modern romance:

1. Single men would prefer being married.
2. Married men actually leave their wives.
3. Men who wear gold chains give gold rings.

The patient will fantasize that, if she only waits long enough, her love object will eventually apologize and say he's changed his mind; everything he said was all a mistake and now he realizes he's more in love than ever before. The patient imagines herself giving the love object a hard time, perhaps hanging up the phone, although, inevitably, she plans to both forgive him and to get an incredibly expensive gift out of the misunderstanding.

When the phone fails to ring, the patient often experiences a compulsive urge to call or write the love object's current girlfriend, wife, mother, or boss; thus signalling a leap into the second stage.

Anger and Depression

Anger and depression (A&D) are the dual components of the second stage. Temper tantrums are frequent and violent, varying according to different individuals, although it is fairly safe to assume that all expensive china should be hidden at this point in the patient's recovery.

During A&D, patients are prone to minor accidents, inflicting superficial damage to various limbs. Stubbed toes, black-and-blue marks, and razor nicks are frequent occurrences. Patients often rediscover the head-banging techniques they originally employed at the age of twenty-seven months. It is best, at this stage, to discourage patients from operating moving vehicles.

Once the anger subsides, depression usually sets in. The patient will feel that life without her love object is simply not worth living. If the patient begins gazing longingly at the kitchen stove or the medicine cabinet, it is wise to hire a twenty-four-hour nurse. During this stage the patient will either cry a lot, sleep eighteen or nineteen hours a day, or watch daytime television.

Self-Pity

The transition into stage three, which Dr. Kahula-Rossi calls the stage of self-pity, is so gradual that it's difficult to distinguish it from depression. Both are characterized by intense absorption in food and beverage. A weight gain of ten to fifteen pounds, or more, is not unusual at this transitional stage.

The major difference, however, is that during the self-pity period, the patient gradually becomes more verbal. While the depression stage is characterized by heavy, prolonged sighing, and the occasional hand-wringing, the self-pity stage sees the patient begin to speak again. Dr. Kahula-Rossi has noted that, while engaged in the self-pity stage, patients are particularly prone to ask rhetorical questions, such as: "Why does this always happen to me?" or "What's wrong with me?" or "I'm a good person, aren't I?"

Explaining this phenomenon, Dr. Kahula-Rossi has written, "It is my theory that since patients are totally self-involved at this stage, they feel quite justified in asking questions that only they, themselves, can answer."

At this stage, it doesn't really matter how you answer the patients' questions. If you agree with their morbid assessment of the world, they'll get sarcastic and say, "Well, you're a big help. I need you like a hole in the head." If you disagree with the patient, he or she will accuse you of patronizing them. Dr. Kahula-Rossi has concluded that patients must work through their own self-pity. "That's why it's called *self*-pity in the first place," notes the astute doctor.

Stop Feeling Hurt

Ultimately, patients get past feeling self-pity when they let go of feeling hurt. They can do this either by falling in love with someone else, by getting born again, or by receiving a negative prognosis from a doctor. Any of these procedures have been known to give patients a new lease on life. However, barring these extremes, the patient may come out of the self-pity stage of her own accord.

Once patients let go of the hurt, they are prepared to fulfill the fifth and most satisfying stage of recovery. They stop concentrating on hurting themselves and start thinking about hurting the love object.

Hurt Someone Else

During this stage, patients will become consumed with plans for revenge. They spend enormous amounts of time and energy concocting ways of making the ex-love object pay through the nose either emotionally or monetarily. If the couple was not married, it is during this stage that women begin asking about palimony.

A classic example of a patient successfully working through the Hurt Someone Else stage is that of author Nora Ephron, who got the very best revenge by writing *Heartburn*, humiliating her ex-husband and making a bushel of money at the same time.

(Although they say living well is the best revenge, they're obviously wrong, as any jilted woman will tell you.)

It is only after some kind of satisfaction is achieved that the patient can enter the sixth and final stage, recovery.

Recovery

It is during this final stage that the patient frees herself from the pain of the past and her fear of the future. With the guidance and support of her therapist, the patient discovers she can go out into the world and start over.

"We try to project how long it'll take a patient to have their next heartbreak," confesses Dr. Kahula-Rossi. "Sometimes, we form a pool. Last week, for instance, I won $435 on one of my manic depressives who constantly falls for alcoholic artists."

Amazingly, the process of falling in love, getting dumped, and recovering from a broken heart can repeat itself throughout the patient's lifetime.

How to Wash That Man Out of Your Hair Without Getting Split Ends

Okay, so the bum left you. He walked out. He's gone. He's history.

You feel bad. Real bad.

You want to know: Is there anything I can do to feel better? Anything, that is, that won't either add five inches to my hips or render me unconscious.

The answer is yes.

I know because I've successfully recovered from two major

heartbreaks, one and a half minor infarctions, and too many of the "Gosh-I-wish-this-would've-worked-out" variety to count.

Experts advise that speed is of the essence in getting over a heartbreaker. Prolonged misery and uninterrupted pining for lost love can result in nasty wrinkles and crow's feet which will severely depreciate your resale value on the open dating market.

Use the following guidelines to zip through your pain and heartache—fast—before *your* tail fins are outdated.

Tip #1: Say, "I Should've Married Roger!"

The first thing I do in my own personal recovery program is to say out loud, "I should've married Roger."

Roger was the guy I dated after college. He was kind, considerate, polite, and never late for anything.

Roger enjoyed celebrating our anniversaries (the day we met, the night we first made love, our first visit to Bloomingdale's) with a bottle of Mateus rosé.

Roger was friendly to all my friends. He brought me flowers and mailed me lots of studio cards. He replaced my broken appliances.

One day he said, "You're the kind of woman who deserves to travel in a chauffeur-driven limousine."

I thought Roger was basically a nice, if somewhat lonely, guy. When I wasn't with him, I appreciated how well he treated me, but when we were together, I had a hard time concentrating and tended to forget almost everything he told me.

Even so, Roger was not discouraged. "I'm here for you,"

Roger would say to me. "I love you, and one of these days you'll feel the same way about me. You'll see."

He frequently talked about marriage.

So, naturally, I dumped Roger for an insurance salesman I met one drunken night in Maxwell's Plum.

Roger took it quite badly. He disappeared for almost thirty-six hours and was discovered wandering aimlessly across the George Washington Bridge.

I felt bad; but not as bad as I felt two weeks later when my Allstate boyfriend drop-kicked me for a ballerina with thighs like tempered steel.

I told myself I had no regrets about the way things had worked out, although that was *after* I told myself, "I should've married Roger," which was about five seconds after my mother told me, "You should've married Roger, you numskull!"

Yet, in truth, dumping Roger was not entirely masochistic on my part. I was never really attracted to him. In fact, when I think about Roger, the main physical characteristics I recall are the enormous amount of black hair on his back and his awful cologne. (When I tell myself I should've married Roger, I leave out the memories of waking up in the morning to sheets covered with hair and pillows reeking of English Leather.)

I think it's safe to assume that every woman has, or had, a Roger in her life; that one really nice guy with a fatal flaw (or two) who was crazy about her.

So, fill in the blank and repeat after me, "I should've married _____."

Now, once you have the reassurance of knowing someone actually wanted to marry you, you can move on to more specific ways of getting over of the bum who didn't.

Tip #2: Get Rid of Everything That Reminds You of Him

Pack all of his things into one suitcase. Call this your "griefcase." Make sure you collect everything that reminds you of him—his toiletries, the mash notes he wrote, the seashells he collected for you at the beach, the portable television you bought for his promotion, the teddy bear he gave you for your birthday, his photographs, the matchbooks and ticket stubs you saved, the silverware and towels you stole from the motel where you spent your first date. Pack all these things away—except for the television, if it's still working.

If there's not enough room for everything in your griefcase, use a "griefcarton" or, if necessary, a "grieftrunk." If you were living with or married to the bum, you may need a "griefvan."

Tip #3: Grieve

Spend the next twenty-four hours wallowing in your grief and self-pity. Immerse yourself in memories of him.

Play all the records and tapes that remind you of him.

Wear the sexy nightgown you bought for that weekend in the mountains.

Mix up a pitcher of his favorite cocktails and reminisce about the last time you two got plastered together.

Sort through every item in your "griefcase." Read every one of his notes, run your fingers over the embossing on his business card, sniffle over every matchbook.

After thirteen or fourteen hours, you'll start to get restless and begin to wonder if the bum is worth all of your suffering.

You will decide he is, and cry for another hour and forty-five minutes.

You will consider suicide and then remember you haven't yet worn those fabulous Joan and David red high heels, so you still have something worth living for.

By the end of the twenty-four-hour period, you will undoubtedly have bored yourself to sleep.

Tip #4: Modify Your Behavior

After your day of grief isolation, you may be fooled into thinking you're over him for good. Be particularly careful, because, like any of your major addictions (alcohol, drugs, cigarettes, *General Hospital*), you can easily fall back into your destructive patterns.

Thus, you need to train yourself to refrain from thinking about him. Psychiatrists call this "behavior modification" and have used the basic technique to train laboratory rats, so, with a little effort, the method will work for you, too.

The procedure is simple: Every time he comes into your mind, run into the kitchen and start chopping an onion.

Work furiously and be sure to keep your face close to the cutting board. (WARNING: Do not use any of those stupid onion-cutting tricks your mom taught you, such as running cold water or sticking a match between your lips.) Continue chopping for ten minutes or until you are crying too hard to see straight.

When you go out, you must take the onions, knife, and cutting board with you. Keep them in your purse, and, if you think about him while driving to the dentist, pull over to the side of the road and chop that onion!

If you punish yourself in this way, you will stop thinking about him well before your second pot of onion soup.

Tip #5: Learn to Cope with the R.A.J.E. Quartet

The R.A.J.E. Quartet is the term psychiatrists have coined to cover the four basic elements of a broken heart: Revenge, Anger, Jealousy, and Envy.

Revenge

Revenge is the healthiest of these emotions and should be encouraged at all times. Spend a lot of time plotting your revenge. Even if you never actually slash his tires, toss rotten eggs at his dog, or leave obscene messages on his answering machine, it's still satisfying to contemplate these activities.

Anger

Anger is a difficult emotion for all of us to handle. Working through our anger provides shrinks with a wellspring of material, along with working through our guilt over sex, which is another story altogether. As the noted psychiatrist, Emil Kohutten has written: "If my patients didn't have such a profoundly difficult time handling their anger, I wouldn't get to drive a new BMW every year."

Jealousy

Jealousy is that one emotion women are most accustomed to dealing with. We are taught, almost from birth, to be jealous of our fellow females. From the first time we attempt to suffocate our newborn baby sister to five minutes ago when we gave serious consideration to tripping the thin blonde standing in front of us at the cash machine, most women accept jealousy as a prerequisite to their daily lives.

Envy

Envy, the fourth and last of the Big Four emotions, is the feeling we most try to deny. We tell ourselves we do not envy anyone else's life, that we are entirely above the emotion.

This, of course, is a whopping big lie.

The truth is we are plagued with thoughts of envy and we strive mightily to evoke the emotion in others.

Consequently, the best way for us to deal with envy is to admit our feelings and accept them as part of who we are.

We can learn how to express our true self by taking a lesson from the world's most legendary heroine when she said, "Oh, Rhett, everyone will be pea-green when they see our house . . . I want everyone who's been mean to me to feel bad."

Right on, Miss Scarlett!

Tip #6: Getting Rid of Split Ends

So, now you've dealt with revenge, anger, jealousy, and envy; you've reminded yourself of all the men who really wanted you (okay, the *man* who really wanted you); you've disposed of all your ex's bikini briefs and other paraphernalia; you've grieved your little heart out; you've changed your pattern of behavior; and you've brushed up on *Gone with the Wind*. In short, you've taken all the steps required to wash that man out of your hair, permanently. Now you are ready to embark, once more, on the road to romance.

Close this book. Take a deep breath.

Open this book to the section, "How to Call a Man for a Date." Begin, again.

Oh, and as for those troublesome split ends. Darling, you treat damaged hair in the same way you treat damaged men. You cut your losses.

Move on to your next fabulous haircut—and your next fantastic man!

Afterword

 For three days after death, hair and fingernails continue to grow, but the phone calls taper off.

—*Johnny Carson*

ESSENCE BALANCING OPPOSING DESIRES.

Stine

Dating Revisited

As I mentioned in the Preface, I began writing this book shortly after getting unceremoniously dumped by Jim.

That was four months ago. At about the same time, I had lunch with my friend, Lisa. Over margaritas, I told Lisa the whole miserable story.

"That schmuck!" said Lisa. "What guy in his right mind would do that to you? Listen, I guarantee, you haven't heard the last from this bozo. He'll call again, you'll see, to tell you he's made a big mistake."

"Gee, Lisa, I don't know."

"Listen to me, I *know* about these things. I've seen it happen a million times. Guys are so dense.

"One day, when you're least expecting it, Jim'll call to say he's picked the wrong woman."

"He said this other woman was a doctor."

"Doctor, schmoctor. A best-selling author beats a stupid M.D. any day."

"He said they met through a singles ad in *New York* magazine."

"Okay, so they've had a romantic beginning; that doesn't mean he won't come to his senses. He'll call and beg you to forgive him. Just give him another chance. He'll whine like mad about going crazy if you two don't get back together again."

"You think?" I said, rather enjoying the image in my mind of Jim on his knees.

"Absolutely," said Lisa. "And it'll be great for your self-esteem when you tell him to screw off."

"Do I have to be so . . . abrupt?"

"You wouldn't actually want to see that slimebucket again, would you?"

"Well . . ."

"Where's your self-respect? Of course you wouldn't want to see him again."

"No, I suppose not."

"Right."

Well, four months have gone by, and here I am, at the end of this book that I'd hoped to conclude with an account of Jim's phone call. The problem is that Jim hasn't called.

Lisa says not to worry. "The longer he waits to call, the bigger a jerk he is. When a guy is really, really stupid it takes him longer to figure out his mistakes. Maybe six months, maybe a year. If this guy's a real boob, it may take a couple of years, but you'll see, he'll call. Eventually."

"Are you sure?"

"You know something, sweetie? If he doesn't call it only means one thing. He's not even man enough to *admit* his mistakes."

For obvious reasons, I enjoy my talks with Lisa and have come to depend on her more and more since the "Jim Incident." We talk on the phone at least once a week, and tonight we're going to the movies together.

During the Coming Attractions, we'll eat popcorn and trash Jim. After the movie, we'll go out to dinner and discuss my feelings about Jim in greater detail, which, as always, will help deepen my understanding that boyfriends may come and go, but friends like Lisa are available on Saturday night.

—Sunshine
Saturday night in June
New York City